Personalizing Learning

Transforming educat⋯ ⋯d

Personalizing Learning

Transforming education for every child

John West-Burnham
and Max Coates

Continuum
11 York Road,
London
SE1 7NX

First published 2005, Reprinted 2007, 2008
© John West-Burnham and Max Coates

ISBN-13: 978 1 85539 114 7
ISBN-10:   1 85539 114 7

Managing editor: Dawn Booth
Design: Heather Blackham
Illustrations: Heather Blackham
Cover design: Marc Maynard

Printed in Great Britain by MPG Books Ltd, Bodmin, Cornwall

Contents

Case studies

About the authors

Greg Barker

Greg Barker is in his fourteenth year of headship. He is a consultant leader and an active member of the Leadership Network of the National College for School Leadership (NCSL). Currently, he is engaged in research on within-school variation.

Max Coates

Max Coates is currently programme director for 'Working Together for Success' for the London Leadership Centre. He is also a regional facilitator for NCSL's New Visions Programme for early headship. He was also researcher for the Evidence for Policy and Practice Information (EPPI) and Co-ordinating Centre review of citizenship education. Other areas of work include mentor coaching, learning and motivation.

Sharon Cousins

Sharon Cousins is an advisory officer with the Southern Education and Library Board (SELB) in Northern Ireland. She has been a teacher and is currently leading research and development projects in thinking skills and assessment for learning, in association with Queen's University Belfast (QUB) and the Council for Curriculum, Examinations and Assessment (CCEA).

Ian McKenzie

Ian McKenzie is the inaugural principal of Kambrya College in Victoria, Australia, a relatively new college, only four years young. Kambrya is an innovative college, investigating deep learning.

Hazel Pulley

Hazel Pulley is the headteacher of Caldecote Community Primary School in Leicester city, her fourth headship in inner-city schools. Hazel is also a consultant leader and key facilitator for the New Visions Programme at the NCSL.

John West-Burnham

John West-Burnham is a teacher, writer and consultant in educational leadership. He is senior visiting research fellow, Centre for Educational Leadership, University of Manchester and senior research adviser at the NCSL.

Introduction

Personalizing learning is emerging as a dominant theme in the reconceptualization of the way in which education is provided. It is a component of the rethinking of the values and ethos underpinning the delivery of public services. At the heart of the personalization debate is recognition of the concept of a *service* provided to *individuals* to meet their specific and personal needs. This represents a profound change from the prevailing orthodoxy of people having to fit into the systems and structures of a bureaucratic system as best they can. It is difficult to be precise about the origins and motivations behind this change. A range of factors can be proposed: increasing dissatisfaction with the public sector; consumerism becoming the dominant factor in our culture; a genuine desire by professionals to enhance the quality of the services they provide; and the loss of a deferential and acquiescent public prepared to be pathetically grateful for any service.

Individual teachers and school leaders have long sought to respond to the needs of the individual learner. In fact, virtually every school's aims or values statement is couched in terms of aspirations for individual success and achievement. However, the reality is very different for most young people in schools. Schools are, by definition, generic experiences; in almost every respect schools are organized in terms of standardized experiences:

- an identical curriculum is delivered to all;

- there is automatic chronological cohort progression, irrespective of individual development;

- the emphasis is on the teaching of the class;

- the school day is standardized and regulated.

Of course there are very good reasons for this approach in terms of efficiency and equity. But it is a denial of the reality of people's lives. At no other time in a person's life is the individual subordinated to the generic as is the norm in schools; in fact choice, diversity and personal freedom are seen as the fundamental criteria for a civilized and meaningful life.

This book argues for the personalization of education through a reconceptualization of the nature of learning, the status of the curriculum and the role of teachers and schools. In essence it advocates a movement from schooling the pupil to educating the learner. It is very important at the outset to distinguish between personalizing learning and individualized learning: the latter carries with it implications of a solitary activity and, as will be demonstrated, personalizing learning is about enhancing learning relationships to optimize the learner's engagement and success. Equally we have taken note of Hargreaves (2004) stricture and refer to personalizing learning rather than personalized learning. The latter implies a misplaced degree of confidence in achieving a very demanding outcome. The fundamental nature of 150 years of social norms and professional practice are being challenged by this.

As authors we are very aware of the care and commitment that teachers demonstrate on a daily basis in supporting the learning and development of young people. We know that right through the education system teachers go to enormous lengths to support individual students – often far in excess of any reasonable professional expectation. Equally we are aware that in many aspects of life in schools the principles of personalization are known and understood, notably in special education and in early years' provision. Our thesis is that young people should not have to depend on the integrity and altruism of individual teachers but rather that the system should be designed around them; hence the use of 'transforming' in our title.

Chapter 1 offers a discussion of the various factors that have led to the current debate about the nature of personalization. Chapter 2 provides a detailed rationale for personalization, while Chapter 3 develops a model of learning to reinforce the rationale. Chapter 4 argues for the curriculum as a process rather than as content. Chapter 5 uses learning styles to develop the focus on the individual. Chapter 6 examines the implications for assessment and Chapter 7 shows how ICT can support the personalization of learning. Chapter 8 considers the implications for our understanding of school leadership.

We are very grateful to Hazel Pulley, Ian McKenzie, Greg Barker and Sharon Cousins for providing material to illuminate key elements of personalization. Many of the ideas in this book were developed in sessions with two National College for School Leadership programmes: the New Visions Programme and the Executive Leadership Programme. We are grateful to all colleagues for the debates and development of ideas. Ingrid Bradbury made the production of this book possible through her expert management of the manuscript.

Max Coates
John West-Burnham

Chapter 1

Understanding personalization

John West-Burnham

The emerging debate about the personalization of learning has its roots in discussions about the nature of education that are as old as the concept of education itself. In essence, the discussion centres on the status of the individual in the educational process – to what extent should the individual fit the system or the system the individual? This tension is at the heart of almost every theory about the structure and content of any education system, and it includes a wide range of fundamental assumptions about the ethical status of the individual, the nature of society, the understanding of the learning process and the nature and purpose of organizations. The interplay of these variables provides one way of explaining the enormous variety of approaches to the process of educating a person both over time and across cultures.

In many ways the debate about personalization can be seen as the latest attempt to restructure the relationship between a range of variables in order to produce an education system that is perceived to be appropriate to a given time and context. In one sense all education systems can be seen as an attempt to reconcile three imperatives: equity, efficiency and excellence (the three 'Es').

- Equity is the dominant imperative in most democratic societies to ensure that access to education is not compromised by poverty, social class, gender, race or learning disability.

- Efficiency refers to the pressure to maximize outcomes (however defined) while minimizing costs – essentially the more for less debate.

- Excellence describes the extent to which an education system is perceived to be achieving high standards of performance.

Much of the deliberation by the state, since the mid-nineteenth century, about the provision of education can be seen as an attempt to optimize these factors. Equally, different cultures have tended to emphasize one of the components at the expense of the others. For many they are in fact irreconcilable – equity and excellence are often seen as mutually exclusive; efficiency will often militate against the other two. Educational policy makers and professionals have long sought to achieve an optimum balance but, almost invariably, the balance is skewed. The reality is shown in Figure 1.1 – equity, efficiency and excellence are only achieved for a minority – the extent to which the three circles overlap might be seen as a judgement on the extent to which a society has achieved a measure of social justice.

For the purposes of this discussion, social justice might be seen as the extent to which a society is inclusive in terms of access to wealth, status, power and, in particular, the levels of

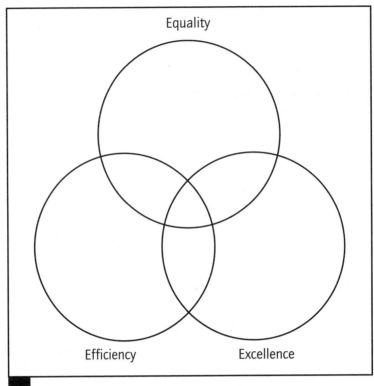

Figure 1.1 Social justice in education systems

participation in all aspects of being a citizen. An obvious example is the right to vote. The extension of the franchise is seen as a key indicator of the extent of democracy and the relative levels of potential social justice. Rawls (2001) captures the central importance of education both as a right in itself and as the means of securing a just society.

> *16.2 If citizens of a well-ordered society are to recognize one another as free and equal, basic institutions must educate them to this conception of themselves, as well as publicly exhibit and encourage this ideal of political justice. This task of education belongs to what we may call the wide role of a political conception. In this role such a conception is part of the public political culture: its first principles are embodied in the institutions of the basic structure and appealed to in their interpretation. Acquaintance with and participation in that public culture is one way citizens learn to conceive of themselves as free and equal, a conception which, if left to their own reflections, they most likely never form, much less accept and desire to realize.* (page 56)

A society that does not promote equity, efficiency and excellence in its education system is unlikely to be perceived by *all* its citizens as promoting democracy, justice and fairness – the fundamental criteria for a good life in our current understanding.

Reconciling equity, efficiency and excellence has to be the goal of every policy maker in a democracy. There is a wealth of evidence to suggest that, in many education systems, attempts to do so at both macro and micro level are failing. As the cost of education continues to rise, there is not a commensurate increase in measurable performance. The socially disadvantaged continue to be systematically marginalized by the structure of school systems. As standards rise, so the debate about excellence is redefined to reinforce elitist models of achievement.

Largely in response to the perceived increasing failure of all branches of the public sector to achieve the three Es, a fundamental rethink of the nature of public services has been taking place. The concept of modernization is increasingly dominating the debate about the future of public services. Newman (2002) identifies the following characteristics of the modernization approach:

- *Managers [are] the agents for delivering the wishes or aspirations of citizens or users.*

- *Organizations designed around the concept of efficiency of use (for example, ease of access, availability of services, and integration of services to localities or client groups).*

- *Open organizational boundaries, well developed networks.*

- *Relations with consumers governed through their participation in service design and planning.*

- *Relations with the public governed through participative or dialogic alongside representative democracy.* (page 87)

A logical extension of these principles is the switch from an emphasis on the supplier to an emphasis on the client. In many ways, the public sector in Britain had reached a level of bureaucratization by the late twentieth century that meant it was more concerned with its own internal integrity than the nature of the service it was originally designed to supply. The public sector had become self-legitimizing, self-validating and self-referential. The stubborn failure of educational standards to rise as a result of government intervention and direction, and a number of tragic examples of the failure of the public services, have led to a rethink of the nature of the public sector.

According to Bentley and Wilsden (2003):

> We still rely on a shared social context that is bigger than ourselves, but we are less ready to submit to standardized relationships with large, impersonal organizations. The more we learn about the factors shaping mobility, achievement, and wellbeing, the clearer it becomes that services that genuinely engage with the particular needs of users are more effective in creating positive outcomes. To use resources effectively, services must be personalized.

> This is the vision that politics should offer; of a public realm that treats each individual as having equal worth by adapting its support to their unique needs and potential. (page 20)

Understanding personalization

The changes in the government of education in England reflect many of the issues and tensions outlined above. Central to the change in the understanding of the role of policy, in creating an education system that is equitable, efficient and excellent, is the concept of personalizing learning. Leadbeater (2004) establishes the fundamental principles for the reform of all public services:

> Public service reform should be user centred. It should be organized to deliver better solutions for the people who use the services. But it must also, in the

process, deliver better outcomes for society as a whole: effective collective provision to meet the need for education, health, transport, community safety and care for vulnerable people. The challenge is to build these two sources of value – for the individual users and the wider society – together. The combination creates public value. (page 6)

He then applies this principle to education:

That is why we need a new framework to show how personal needs can be taken into account within universal equity and excellence in education. Of course everyone wants an education system that is both equitable and excellent. In recent years the policy agenda has grown to recognize the fact that in the context of greater diversity we can only understand these terms by putting the needs and wants of individual learners at the heart of the system. (page 6)

This view was politically endorsed by David Miliband, former Minister for School Standards, at the North of England Education Conference in 2004.

High expectations of every child, given practical form by high quality teaching based on a sound knowledge and understanding of each child's needs. It is not individualized learning where pupils sit alone. Nor is it pupils left to their own devices – which too often reinforces low aspirations. It means shaping teaching around the way different youngsters learn; it means taking the care to nurture the unique talents of every pupil.

This builds on his statement in 2003 (quoted in Hargreaves (2004)):

 Personalizing learning demands that every aspect of teaching and support is designed around a pupil's needs.

Hargreaves (2004) himself identifies the challenge thus:

… can more be done to meet the learning needs of all *students?*

So personalized learning is a process that:

- *reinforces some current practices in schools and classrooms*

- *demands modifications to some of these practices*

- *entails creating some new practice*

- *personalization may be treated as a version of what is called* customization *in the business world.* (page 5)

The Department for Education and Skills (2004b) has identified a range of principles to inform 'day-to-day' practice.

For pupils it means:

- having their individual needs addressed, both in school and extending beyond the classroom and into the family and community;

- coordinated support to enable them to succeed to the full, whatever their talent or background;

- a safe and secure environment in which to learn, with problems effectively dealt with;

- a real say about their learning.

For parents and carers it means:

- regular updates, that give clear understanding of what their child can currently do, how they can progress and what help can be given at home;

- being involved in planning their children's future education;

- the opportunity to play a more active role in school life and know that their contribution is valued.

For teachers it means:

- high expectations of every learner, giving the confidence and skills to succeed;

- access to and use of data on each pupil, informing teaching and learning, with more time for assessment and lesson planning;

- opportunities to develop a wide repertoire of teaching strategies, including information and communications technology (ICT);

- access to a comprehensive continuing professional development (CPD) programme.

For schools it means:

- a professional ethos that accepts and assumes every child comes to the classroom with a different knowledge base and skill set, as well as having varying aptitudes and aspirations;

- a determination for every young person's needs to be assessed and their talents developed through diverse teaching strategies.

Hargreaves (2004: page 7) identifies nine gateways to personalizing learning:

- learning to learn

- assessment for learning

- new technologies

- advice and guidance

- mentoring

- student voice

- organization

- workforce

- curriculum.

Hargreaves (2004) goes on to explain how personalization might work:

> *So entry to personalized learning may be made through any one of these nine gateways: starting from one gateway soon leads to one or more of the others ... The fact that these gateways are interlinked is an advantage, for though networks of schools or teachers may start in one gateway, they are soon led to different ones, from which other networks started their innovation journey.*
>
> *This can produce an overall, coherent version of personalization as a well of recourses from which everyone can draw. We cannot specify – and should not seek – a formal definition of personalization before we embark on the journeys of these innovation networks. We shall discover what personalization is during the journey itself.* (page 10)

There is no one definitive view as to what personalization actually means in theory, let alone in practice. However, on the basis of the broad principles identified above it may be possible to identify some core propositions about the nature of personalization:

- Services are designed in response to the defined needs of clients.

- Clients are active participants in the management of services.

- The internal structures and processes of services are designed to facilitate access and engagement by clients.

- Clients are partners in the design and development of future provision.

- The primary accountability of providers is to clients.

- Clients are able to make valid, self-directed choices.

Hargreaves' caution against a contrived or imposed definition of personalizing is wise, as is his stricture against personalized learning – seeing personalizing learning as an emergent process rather than using an artificially imposed definition. However, it is appropriate to explore the motivation for personalization, as the conceptual framework that guides the process will, inevitably, determine the shape of the final model that is applied.

At this stage it is appropriate to distinguish between the personalization of learning and individualized learning. Again, it is a matter of semantics but, in the context of this discussion, the individualization of learning is seen as those strategies that focus on the learner working in isolation – using an individualized learning programme or (as in the nightmare scenario) only interacting with a computer screen. E.M. Forster, in his short story *The Machine Stops*, published in 1909, captures the ultimate expression of individualization:

> *Then she generated the light, and the sight of her room, flooded with radiance and studded with electric buttons, revived her. There were buttons and switches everywhere – buttons to call for food, for music, for clothing. There was the hot-*

bath button, by pressure of which a basin of (imitation) marble rose out of the floor, filled to the brim with a warm deodorized liquid. There was the cold-bath button. There was a button that produced literature. And there were of course the buttons by which she communicated with her friends. The room, though it contained nothing, was in touch with all that she cared for in the world.

The clumsy system of public gatherings had been long since abandoned; neither Vashti nor her audience stirred from their rooms. Seated in her armchair she spoke, while they in their armchairs heard her, fairly well, and saw her fairly well. (page 5)

To talk of learning alone is to deny the central feature of learning – that it is based in social relationships. Even the most basic neurological process is conditioned by the environment. Personalization is about enhancing the status of the individual so that learning in social contexts is more effective.

There are multiple routes to personalization, but they can be clustered into three main categories:

- the status of the individual in society;
- the nature of the learning process;
- the role of the organization.

The status of the individual in society

In many ways, education is the process by which society replicates itself. The purpose of education is to ensure the perpetuation of knowledge, values and beliefs, and central to these is the significance that is attached to the role and status of the individual. In ant colonies the survival of the genetic inheritance is a more powerful factor than the integrity of any one individual. Human history can be seen as very uneven progress towards the ideal of each person having value in his or her own right. The debate about personalization in education can be seen as a significant component of a broader dialogue about the value that is ascribed to each person.

Perhaps the most pervasive and influential view of the dominance of the rights of society over the individual is that of Plato – described by Popper in the following terms:

Because of his radical collectivism, Plato is not even interested in those problems which men usually call the problems of justice, that is to say, in the impartial weighing of the contesting claims of individuals. [...] Justice, to him, is nothing but the health, unity and stability of the collective body. (Corvi, 1997: page 59)

The subordination of the individual to a higher, collective good reaches its ultimate expression in Huxley's (1932) dystopia, *Brave New World*:

'And that,' put in the Director sententiously, 'that is the secret of happiness and virtue – liking what you've got to do. All conditioning aims at that: making people like their unescapable social destiny.' (page 12)

For Plato, and in Huxley's world, the purpose of education is to subordinate the individual to collective needs and norms. There are, however, equally compelling arguments that reverse this approach; for Rousseau in *Emile* an education that focuses on the individual results in a situation where:

> *It is then only that he finds his true interest in being good, in acting rightly without thought of the applause of men, and, without being forced by the laws, in being just in all matters between God and himself ... (Claydon, 1969)*

Rousseau's naive optimism is posited on a paradoxical formula – freedom through compliance – but he did provide the most powerful case for challenging the social predestination of the masses and, in starting with the individual, provided a major corrective to the orthodoxy of education as preparation for subordination. The answer, of course, lies between the two extremes. For Gardner (1999b) there are the polarities of 'uniform and individualized education'; at one extreme is the uniformity found in many systems:

> *Standing in opposition is an individualized perspective that highlights the vast differences among individuals' strengths, needs, goals. It makes sense to construct an education that takes into account these differences among persons. Perhaps, indeed, such an education is fairer; it does not valorize a certain kind of mind but rather meets each student where he or she is. Nor does such an education mandate that each person should come to resemble others in the community. In contrast to a Lockean view: that the individual should be shaped according to the designs of the community, the 'Rousseauian' view would allow the natural inclinations of the human individual to unfold and endure. (page 37)*

In concluding his study, Gardner (1999b) makes a plea for an approach to education that allows individuals to create their own understanding of the world, but:

> *First, understanding is difficult to achieve, and the obstacles to its attainment are formidable. Second, possessing different kinds of minds, individuals represent information and knowledge in idiosyncratic ways. In the future, if education is to achieve greater success with more individuals, it ought to affirm and build upon these two considerations. (page 245)*

If it is to be more than educational consumerism (every learner with their own educational supermarket trolley) personalization has to be rooted in a deep respect for the integrity, dignity and validity of each person. Personalization then has the potential to both enhance the individual's learning and provide the vehicle to deepen, enrich and sustain that individuality.

Personalization has enormous potential to humanize schools if it is deeply committed to realizing the capacity of every individual to grow, develop and learn. Without a deep commitment to the uniqueness of each person it could become an exercise in bureaucratic managerialism. Above everything else, personalization is a morally driven strategy:

> *To build a successful system of personalized learning, we must begin by acknowledging that giving every single child the chance to be the best they can be, whatever their talent or background, is not the betrayal of excellence, it is the fulfilment of it. Personalized learning means high quality teaching that is responsive to the different ways students achieve their best. There is a clear moral and educational case for pursuing this approach. A system that responds*

to individual pupils, by creating an education path that takes account of their needs, interests and aspirations, will not only generate excellence, it will also make a strong contribution to equity and social justice. (Department for Education and Skills, 2004a)

The nature of the learning process

If personalization is a moral imperative then it is equally driven by practical considerations. Schooling as a social process emerged in the late nineteenth and early twentieth centuries in a culture of deference, dependence and compliance. The vast majority of the population was prepared for lives in factories, on farms, as servants and to be slaughtered in thousands at the whim of incompetent generals. This was all possible in a society that believed in a natural hierarchy of ability and saw an individual's potential being fixed and determined at birth. There are many aspects of schooling that still echo this world view.

Personalization of learning offers a powerful opportunity to design education systems around a totally different conceptual framework that is based on scientific and social research rather than pseudo-science and social prejudice.

The nature of learning is the core theme of this book, and it is considered in detail in Chapter 3. At this stage, therefore, it is appropriate to offer some key propositions that relate learning to personalization.

- **Each learner is unique**

  Irrespective of a vast range of shared social experiences, each of us has a unique set of life experiences that determine our distinctiveness as people. Every parent knows that, given a wide range of totally consistent factors, each of his or her children will be a distinctive and unique human being. The interplay of genetic, neurological, physiological and social factors conspires to give us an astonishing range of permutations.

- **Learning is neurological**

  Learning is a physical process in the brain – it is the result of an amazingly complex series of interactions that we are only just beginning to understand. Winston (2003) captures this by asking his readers to imagine two human brains:

  There would be nothing to reveal that these two rubber objects, which to some bystanders would seem faintly disgusting, respectively comprised the sum total of our very being and personality. Nothing to show that at some time we had both loved in different ways, had known different pains, ambitions and disappointments, and had been angry and taken pleasure at different things. Nor that we had learnt different physical and intellectual skills, had mind-bending experiences in different parts of the world, had totally different memories, liked different food or music, and that each of us had quite different human strengths and failings. (pages 1–2)

  If personalization is to be more than superficial choices it has to recognize the neurological basis of learning.

- ## Intelligence can be learned

An extension of the neurological basis of learning is coming to terms with our genetic inheritance. For much of human history it was assumed that intelligence, however defined, was largely inherited. However, just as each of us has a unique DNA profile so we have a unique profile of abilities: the result of astonishingly complex interaction. This is a highly contested area for Pinker (2002):

> *... there is now ample evidence that intelligence is a stable property of an individual, that it can be linked to features of the brain (including overall size, amount of grey matter in the frontal lobes, speed of neural conduction, and metabolism of cerebral glucose), that it is partly heritable among individuals, and that it predicts some of the variation in life outcomes such as income and social status.* (page 150)

Ridley (2003) argues:

> *The main conclusion of behaviour genetics is counter-intuitive in the extreme. It tells you that nature plays a role in determining personality, intelligence and health – that genes matter. But it does not tell you that this role is at the expense of nurture. If anything, it proves rather dramatically that nurture matters just as much, though it is inevitably less good at discerning how ... Nature does not prevail over nurture; they do not compete; they are not rivals; it is not nature versus nurture at all.* (page 93)

And he concludes his study:

 Nature versus nurture is dead. Long live nature via nurture.

(Ridley, 2003: page 280)

It may be, as knowledge grows, that, in generations to come, personalization will start with an individual's genetic profile – as is just beginning to be possible in medicine. While IQ may be relatively fixed, the other intelligences are amenable to a wide range of variables.

- ## Learning as an emotional experience

How are you feeling today? Has reading this book made you happy, sad, irritated, excited, frustrated, challenged or bored? Your engagement with our writing will be the result of many factors outside of our control – relationships at work, at home, your hopes for your career, your personal values system or your professional experience. This book was written in a range of emotional states and will be read in a range of emotional states – nobody can be objective about this book.

And so it is in every learning situation – our emotions will have a profound and abiding impact on who we are and how we learn. Classrooms are emotional cauldrons and every experienced teacher will know the impact that their behaviour will have on the behaviour of the class.

In some ways emotions are the doorways to learning – even if everything else is propitious then a dysfunctional emotional state or inappropriate relationships will ensure that the doors remain closed. The good news, according to Goleman (1996), is:

While purely cognitive capacities remain relatively fixed, emotional competence can be learned at any point in life. No matter how insensitive, shy, hot-tempered, awkward, or tuned-out people may be, with motivation and the right effort they can cultivate emotional competence.(pages 240–241)

If we are serious about personalization then we have to be aware of the individual's emotional state as much as any other factor.

One of the great dangers with personalization is that it will be in terms of teacher behaviour, for example more time spent with individuals, than actually focusing on who the individuals are. This leads naturally to the third element in this section – the relationship between the individual and the organization.

The role of the organization

Imagine making your normal weekly trip to the supermarket. When you walk in everything has changed – the shelves have gone and have been replaced by rows of full baskets and trolleys.

An assistant explains:

'Sorry for any confusion. It's just that it was very expensive and time consuming for us to keep filling the shelves and check out each item. So we have prepared your shopping in advance, we know exactly what goods are going out and how much each basket costs. We all save time and money.'

'But how do you know what I need?' you protest.

'Well there are nine types of basket or trolley – upper, middle and lower class (expensive, medium and cheap). We are certain that you will find a basket close to your needs. It is important to remember how this helps us to offer an efficient service!'

Such a scenario is clearly nonsense; the whole point of going to the supermarket is choice. Your satisfaction with your chosen supermarket is the extent to which you are able to find all the items on your shopping list. And so it is with almost every aspect of our lives, we expect choice and our view of any product or service is the extent to which our needs are met. Hargreaves (2004) draws a precise parallel between personalization and customization and compares the Model T Ford motor car with those produced by the Japanese motor industry. The success of the Japanese car makers is explained by their ability to mass produce choice and to do so with high quality and reasonable cost.

The key difference between Japanese manufacturers and their European and American counterparts in the 1970s and 1980s was the philosophy of total quality. Total quality is a management philosophy based on a very simple premise: quality is achieved by customer or client needs.

This premise switches the emphasis from the supplier to the customer – quality is not an abstract, absolute ideal but is rather the extent to which a product or service is 'fit for purpose', where the purpose is defined by the customer. Thus a quality car is not necessarily a Rolls-Royce; it is a car that meets the needs of the owner. Equally, a quality lesson or learning experience is not one that meets the needs of the teacher ('Taught my best ever lesson today – pity the children weren't ready for it') but rather the needs of the learner. However beautifully crafted a lesson, if it is not fit for purpose then it is a failure.

The total quality movement required a complex change of organizational culture – and was notoriously difficult to apply in British organizations. The pivotal principles of the total quality movement might be defined as:

- fitness for purpose – quality is defined by customer needs;

- customers are integrated into the design of goods and services;

- an emphasis on prevention – stopping things going wrong;
  quality assurance rather than inspection;

- suppliers constantly trying to improve the product or service – 'delighting
  the customer'.

The principles of personalization are well understood in a commercial and industrial context. In many ways, personalization in education is simply catching up with a change in expectations that has dominated our economic lives for several years now. This is not to argue for the simplistic transfer of industrial techniques into schools, but rather to urge that education has the opportunity to come to terms with an organizational culture that is well understood by all those involved in the governance, leadership and teaching in schools; they all expect a quality approach in every other aspect of their lives.

Possible practical implications of personalizing learning

It would be wrong to try and specify the precise nature of what personalization means in education. However, on the basis of the principles established in this chapter and what is already known about successful practice, any movement towards personalizing learning will need to take the following factors into account. This list provides a broad agenda for the rest of this book.

- The diagnosis and profiling of learning styles, aptitudes, dispositions and preferences supported by the development of meta-cognitive understanding.

- The development of a 'cognitive curriculum', for example cognitive strategies – problem solving, analytical thinking, creativity, reasoning, organizing information, memory, persistence and, crucially, negotiation and choice.

- The development of social learning skills, for example listening, co-operation and collaboration, small group learning, team learning and negotiation.

- Access to mentoring and coaching and development as a mentor and coach. (Use of *all* adults in the school as mentors plus non-school based adults and students.) Mentoring to focus on the management of individual learning plans (pathways).

- Extending choice in the curriculum by changing the definition of a curriculum to a range of learning processes rather than formalized content.

- Use of ICT to ensure continuous access to learning.

- Building flexibility into the school experience so that there is choice as to what, when, where and how something is learned.

- The creation of sophisticated monitoring, consultative and participatory strategies to ensure student engagement in learning, and student voice in the development of learning-centred schools.

- The development of flexible assessment strategies, assessment for learning.

The reality of personalizing learning is perhaps best captured by Christopher Bowring-Carr in his cameos of two learners in Bowring-Carr and West-Burnham (1997):

> 'Let me see.' He opened the file on Marianne, and saw that she had 'time-out' three months ago to finalize a module in science. She had completed the module, and done very well in the examination that she chose to do straight afterwards, and then had successfully caught up with her other work. 'That looks good, Marianne. At the end of this session, would you go and make contact with your coach and see if he can help at all.' (page 6)

> After the tutorial, Judith went home to settle down to complete writing a paper (the old term stuck tenaciously). She had to get it to her drama teacher in time for him to read it and then they and the other four in the group would discuss it at the next session. The deadline was that afternoon. Being on cable, she could work from home without any difficulty. For those who had not got that facility, the school had set up study carrels, both in the main building and in outreach centres, which were open for 18 hours a day, and were always well used. She worked until 12.00, and then went back to the drama studio to meet Ellen for her weekly 'one-to-one'. (page 11)

> Judith walked over to room 18, where she was to meet her buddy. Many of the older students volunteered to meet on a weekly basis with a younger student as part of the coaching and mentoring programme. She liked Ahmed enormously, and the two of them looked forward to their weekly meeting. He had brought with him the book he was reading at the time, and they started off by him reading a passage.

> 'That's great,' said Judith. 'Not a single mistake. But your voice is still pretty flat. You don't sound as if you're really involved with what you're reading.' (page 17)

In his fictionalized account about the life of a learner, Bowring-Carr demonstrates a number of key features of personalization:

- student choice supported by advice;

- coaching and mentoring;

- multiple learning opportunities;

- collaborative planning of what to learn and how to learn it.

Underpinning all of these points is a deep respect for learners, based on trust and recognition of their value as unique human beings.

Chapter 2

A changing world

John West-Burnham

There is overwhelming evidence that points to the inappropriateness of the existing system of schools and to as what is needed to replace it. This chapter offers an essentially pessimistic view of global trends most of which, though not all, will have only limited impact on this book's authors and readership. The chances are that the majority of us are of an age, having social status and economic security, that will shield us from some of the changes – except those that are directly to our benefit. However, the very fact that you are reading this book indicates a professional and so a moral commitment to education as a social process which is founded on the belief that we as teachers are committed to the preparation of young people to live fulfilling, secure, safe and creative lives. The crucial issue is: to what extent does a school system, rooted in the nineteenth century, adequately prepare people for life in the twenty-first century? In one sense chronological dates are irrelevant, but they are symbolic of significant trends that the rest of this chapter will explore. These trends are: the new scientific paradigm; the information revolution; the nature of society; work and the economy; and a fragile world.

A powerful model that illustrates the rate of change is the time taken to run the four-minute mile. In 1913 the record stood at four minutes 14.4 seconds. Roger Bannister broke the four-minute barrier in 1954 with a time of three minutes 59.4 seconds. Since 1954 the record has been broken 18 times. Once the barrier was broken (and it was thought to be physically impossible to break it), rapid improvement became the norm. At the time of writing, the record stands at three minutes 43.13 seconds. Once change is initiated it can grow exponentially.

The new scientific paradigm

Since the eighteenth century, science has increasingly shaped our world view, replacing theological interpretation with scientific explanation. In turn, that scientific explanation has moved from universifiability and certainty into ambiguity and contingency. The classic simplicity of Newtonian mechanics, in which everything either was designed or could be designed (the teleological universe), has been replaced by an awareness of complexity, interdependence and integration (the quantum universe). Historic certainties have been replaced by a focus on evolutionary thinking: the emergent has replaced the mechanistic. As Zohar (1997) expresses it:

> We live largely in a world of Newtonian organizations. These are organizations that thrive on certainty and predictability. They are hierarchical ... They are heavily bureaucratic and rule bound ... They stress the single point of view ... They are managed as though the part organizes the whole.

The radically new science of the twentieth century – relativity, quantum mechanics, chaos and complexity theories – helps us to see the basic outlines of the new paradigm ... this new science sharply focuses the associated shift ... It provides us with the new concepts, new categories, new language and new images that new paradigm thinking requires. (page 5)

Manifestations of this new paradigm are found in the way that scientific research is carried out and in the way we approach the arts, critique literature, understand society and view leadership and management – but not, so far, education and the curriculum.

The prevailing school system is essentially Newtonian: hierarchical, simplistically causal and compartmentalized. It is a classic manifestation of the rationalistic fallacy – because something is structured it is coherent. The systematic structure of the curriculum is beguiling, but it is the product of an outdated mindset. Not only has the scientific paradigm changed but also the scientific framework that informs curriculum design. For a century, education has been a derivative discipline drawing on sociology, philosophy and psychology to create an often bizarre synthesis. Education has always been deferential to the social sciences but has only ever sought to teach the natural sciences. The new scientific paradigm offers the promise (or threat) of an education system that is increasingly based on scientific research. The implications of neurological science are discussed in detail in Chapter 3, but this theme provides a classic model of how historical insight, habituated practice and social expectation will be challenged by a new paradigm based on research into brain functioning. This shift is being paralleled by a redefinition of intelligence derived from neurological research. It is worth reflecting on the flawed work on intelligence by the social science approach of Cyril Burt and his contemporaries compared with the research carried out by Howard Gardner. The latter is both scientifically more rigorous and more reflective of the complexity of a human being's intelligences.

When combined with the Human Genome Project, neurological research points to a future of what might be termed scientific individualism. Such individualization heralds a social and educational revolution unless policy makers and educationalists deny the validity and the applicability of the science, or wait for a generation before changing anything. The full implications of the Human Genome Project will take decades to unravel and even longer to turn into practical medicine, but already research into asthma and autism is being transformed through the use of knowledge gained from genetics research. For how long will educationalists be able to perpetuate nineteenth-century models of intelligence and ignore the research into the gene called *IGFzR*? Intelligence will always be culturally defined and genetic dispositions will always be mediated by environment, but genetic depositions will equally be created by the environment – natural selection is manifested, to a significant degree, through genetic make-up. Just as the work of Galileo, Newton and Darwin opened doors that are still shaping scientific discovery, so the Human Genome Project has opened a door, but what path that door opens on to is still uncertain. For Ridley (1999):

I genuinely believe that we are living through the greatest intellectual moment in history. Bar none ... There is much, much more to each of us than a genetic code. But until now human genes were almost a complete mystery. We will be the first generation to penetrate that mystery. We stand on the brink of great new answers but, even more, of great new questions. (page 5)

Some of the answers and questions emerge from the following implications of the Human Genome Project:

- There is no scientific basis for race. Humans share 99 per cent of their DNA (deoxyribonucleic acid).

- Personalized medicine becomes a real possibility.

- 1,778 genes identified with specific diseases have been found so far.

- Jet lag and sleep disorders have genetic origins.

- It will be possible to engineer cells that will hunt down cancer cells.

- There may be the potential to modify an unborn baby's DNA inheritance.

This list could go on and findings from the Human Genome Project will probably introduce new issues at an exceptional rate. There are two important points to emerge from this discussion. First, our understanding of what it means to be human is changing dramatically and so, potentially, is our ability to cure and to change. Second, social and moral issues will move into a new dimension – young people in school today will have to answer questions that we cannot even begin to conceptualize. One significant example of this is that not only will there be racism and sexism to contend with, but there could also be discrimination based on genetic profiles.

There are, of course, many other areas of scientific research that will produce profound changes in the shape of things to come. Genetically modified food, nanotechnology, new materials; these changes and many others will impact on almost every aspect of our lives and will continue to increase in number at an exponential rate – innovation accelerates innovation with a multiplier effect. Any graph tracking the rate of scientific and technological change since humans first started to settle in agricultural communities would show a millennia of barely perceptible movements and then, from the eighteenth century, the lines start an upward trend that currently are near vertical.

The information revolution

Just as there has been an explosion in the creation of scientific knowledge so has there been an explosion in our ability to process information. Indeed, the two are inextricably linked; the Human Genome Project would have been impossible without the power of modern computers. Postulating the long-term impact and implications of information and communications technology (ICT) is almost impossible. However, it is possible to point to a range of trends and extrapolate from them. It is also worth reflecting on the nature of change in ICT: growth is exponential and cumulative. Moore's law says that computer power doubles every 18 months, and each new development accelerates the potential for future developments. Consider a pocket calculator of the early 1970s: it could do the four basic arithmetic functions and cost about £30. Consider the computing power of a £30 calculator today. Equally, think back to the early mobile phones (which were mobile only for the strong and able bodied) and compare them with what is available today – ten per cent of the size and enormously more powerful. The changes have been dramatic, but they have become commonplace because as power and sophistication have increased so the cost has fallen, and so a technological miracle becomes a 'throw-away'.

Examples of this technological explosion include:

- It took 34 years for radio to be available in 50 million homes; it took the internet four years to achieve the same coverage.

- In 2000, IBM introduced Blue Gene – a computer that has 1,000 times the capacity of Deep Blue, which beat the world chess champion, and is two million times more powerful than a desktop PC.

- A watch with the computing power of an early Apple PC, a five-alarm appointment manager, to-do list and phone book is now available.

- By 1915, the American transcontinental telephone system had developed the capacity to handle three simultaneous voice calls. By the 1990s, individual Telstar satellites had enough capacity for nearly 100,000 telephone links.

- Hewlett-Packard Company, in 1998, claimed 58 million people in the United States and Europe are 'mobile professionals' with a need to scan and fax contracts, newspaper articles and market reports while they are on the move.

The implications of this revolution for education are a long way from being fully understood let alone implemented. In most schools ICT has been an adjunct: a better and more efficient way of doing existing things rather than reconceptualizing what should, and now can, be done. In many ways ICT has tended to reinforce shallow learning (see Chapter 3) by focusing on information retrieval and presentation rather than on the creation of knowledge.

ICT has the potential to change the geography, the architecture and the timing of learning. Schools are buildings designed to serve a designated area. They are internally organized on a factory system in which the students are grouped solely by age or subject specialization for a specified number of hours and days each year. ICT renders that model obsolete but, and this is the danger of graduated assimilation, it is used to reinforce the status quo and never realizes its full potential. A classic example of the incremental approach to ICT is the often-voiced anxiety about ICT compromising social relationships in schools. Such an idea reflects a classic misapprehension; it is automatically assumed that children will be in the same relationship with computers as historically they have been with teachers, in other words passive and directed. It also assumes that good-quality social relationships exist now, which is not always the case, and it marginalizes the importance of self-directed learning and ignores the enormous potential of ICT for collaborative learning. This is not to say that there are not real problems with the application of ICT to learning; these are explored in detail in Chapter 7.

The nature of society

There can be no doubt that society, and our understanding of what constitutes society, has changed and will continue to change. If education is partly about preparing young people for life in society, then the curriculum must reflect that society. Again, it is difficult to be totally confident about the sustainability of trends but an overview would lead to the conclusion:

This period, from roughly the mid-1960s to the early 1990s, was marked by seriously deteriorating social conditions in most of the industrialized world. Crime and social disorder began to rise ... the decline of kinship as a social institution ... accelerated sharply. Fertility in most European countries and Japan fell ... Marriages and births became fewer ... Finally, trust and confidence in institutions went into a deep, forty-year decline. (Fukuyama, 1995: page 5)

Fukuyama goes on to argue that, in the US, there are some signs of revival of optimism in the infrastructure of society. Putnam (2000) is equally cautious but is quite clear that there has been, what he calls, 'civic disengagement' or a decline in community involvement that is measured through such factors as political participation, religious affiliation and engagement, volunteering, informal work-based networks and even connectedness in the home. All point to a diminution in 'social capital' – the glue that binds society. One of the key manifestations of Fukuyama's disruption or Putnam's disengagement is the emergence of what might be called ethical and moral relativity. This change reflects exactly, both chronologically and conceptually, the broad growth in scientific understanding outlined at the start of this chapter.

The changes in the essential infrastructure of societies are often most clearly manifested in the loss of an ethical hegemony – the loss of a single authoritative source of guidance as to the basis of belief. This inevitably leads to moral ambiguity as multiple interpretations become possible. Often such changes are liberalizing and humanizing or, from an alternative perspective, mark the end of civilization. The nature of ethical education has moved from 'command and control' to a pseudo-rationalism based on evidence that is garnered from a comparatively local and peer consensus. The impact of social change may well point to the end of such a consensus except that which is enforceable by law, which is not the basis for an ethical society.

Quite apart from this overarching process of change, there are some very specific issues. The first of these is that Western societies are ageing; by the year 2006, the number of people in the UK who have retired will exceed the number of school-age children for the first time. The current school generation will probably be the longest lived in history and will have the potential to enjoy better health throughout longer lives. This longevity has profound implications for a curriculum that was designed for a life of 40 years of work and, with luck, five to ten years in retirement. With changes in the pattern of working, it is not unreasonable to anticipate active retirement of 30 to 40 years. This change is a real challenge to a curriculum that focuses on work. Although the population of the Western world is ageing and in decline this is not true for the planet as a whole. On current UN (United Nations) estimates, the population of the world, six billion in 2000, will have risen to nine billion by 2030. The significant growth will be in Africa, Asia and South America. This fact raises a range of issues around the current patterns of consumption of the world's resources and the capacity of developing countries to actually feed, accommodate and employ such a population.

There are both moral and practical issues emerging from this change in the balance of the world's population, not the least of which is the increasing polarization of societies between the rich and the poor. In essence, the rich are getting richer and the poor are staying poor for the most part. The wealthiest 500 people in the US have more capital than does the entire poorest half of the world's population. One billion people attempt to live on a dollar a day. In Britain, in 1979, five million people lived in poverty and by 1990 that figure had increased to 14 million. Today, about 28 per cent of children in Britain live in relative poverty. Of the world's 23 wealthiest nations, the UK is twentieth in the league table of child poverty – only Italy, the

US and Mexico have more children living in poverty. In the UK, 1.2 million children have been moved out of poverty between 1997 and 2001, but this does not imply that they are now economically secure – they are less poor. The reality in Britain, and in many of the wealthiest nations on earth, is that of the continued existence of an underclass, described by Adonis and Pollard (1997) as:

> ... a product of helplessness, hopelessness, poor single-parenthood (almost invariably single-motherhood) and educational failure. (page 13)

> ... the word underclass captures the essence of the class predicament for many at the bottom; a complete absence of ladders, whether basic skills, role models, education or a culture of work. (page 16)

There is an absolute correlation between economic and social factors, and a child's educational and life chances. The three most significant factors influencing educational success are: poverty, family life and the prevailing level of social capital. The current system of schooling serves to reinforce and exacerbate these factors as success in educational terms is measured in terms that are highly culturally specific. The education system of England has been characterized as 'high on excellence and low on equity' and as having 'the longest tail of underachievement in Europe'. This may be explained by the figure for child poverty in the UK and, for example, the average level of child poverty for the Scandinavian countries of three per cent. Poverty can be directly linked with dysfunctional family life, as Desforges (2003) demonstrates: in the primary years of schooling the family is six times more significant than the school in determining educational success. If the quality of community life is added into the equation, (in other words, the level of social capital) then for some children the odds would seem to be totally against them.

> ... child development is powerfully shaped by social capital ... trust, networks, and norms of reciprocity within a child's family, school, peer group, and larger community have wide-ranging effects on the child's opportunities and choices and, hence, on behaviour and development. (Putnam, 2000)

> States that score high on the social Capital Index are the same states where children flourish. (Putnam, 2000)

> ... social Capital is second only to poverty in the breadth and depth of its effects on children's lives. (Putnam, 2000)

> We can conclude with some confidence that there is a close relationship between people's social networks and their educational performance. (Field, 2003: page 37)

> Overall, outcomes in deprived areas are worse than those in non-deprived areas, whether they are measured in terms of qualification, attendance or exclusions. (Power et al., 2002: page 9)

The link between social disadvantage and educational underachievement is a powerful vindication of the idea of polarization in many societies – and it is also reflected on a global scale. The disparity between rich and poor, advantaged and disadvantaged, is reinforced by a model of schooling that benefits those who have social and cultural characteristics that predispose them to benefit from prevailing educational norms. Personalization may offer a strategy to counteract this imbalance by enhancing the ability of individuals to engage with the school system. Paradoxically, personalization may offer the most powerful antidote to a malaise in society that Neuberger (2005) characterizes in the following terms:

> *For we are individuals now. We demand things. We go for the personal. We understand our own needs. The idea that we might not be able to have what we believe we want and need is anathema to us. We have become demanders, not citizens; we look to ourselves rather than to society as a whole.* (page xviii)

A major issue for curriculum design and development is surely to move away from the myth of the curriculum as an enabler when in fact it is symbolic of all that divides and inhibits. The curriculum, and by that term we mean all that the child experiences in the school, filtered and influenced by what they bring to the school, needs to focus on enabling and encouraging the child to learn, to understand the processes of learning, and to question. Our children need to learn to question because first they are confronted by a torrent of information and the only way they are going to make any sense of it is through being able to ask the right questions and sift and sort the answers. Second, they need to be able to redress the imbalance in society where power is located with those who ask the questions and so determine the answers.

The key social issues that any future model of education will, therefore, have to address would seem to include:

- a society in which more people live longer with retirement becoming a central rather than a marginal social category;

- a society in which poverty and social disadvantage are endemic and where education can, in many cases, no longer be seen as a panacea;

- a society that is increasingly not at ease with itself but rather is marked by disengagement and disillusionment;

- a society that is increasingly morally ambiguous and ethically uncertain;

- a global society that is riven by gross disparities, and in which large minorities see violence as their only possible resource.

Work and the economy

Futurology is a dangerous business and nowhere more so than in predicting the future of work. The claims for the paperless office have long since disappeared under mountains of paper. The anticipated retirement age of 45 has been replaced by the reality of working to 65 or 70 – but still being able to expect a long, productive and active retirement.

However, there are some trends that are clearly established. For example, in Britain in 1970 over 500,000 people worked in the coal and steel industries; today that figure is less than 50,000. What were once perceived as 'bedrock' industries have effectively disappeared from many parts of the UK. Manufacturing industry has seen a steady and significant move of jobs to the developing world. At the same time there has been a steady growth in jobs in the service industries, notably retailing.

The economic balance of many Western economies is changing with an increasing emphasis on a minority of the population engaged in high-value, high reward, knowledge-based work and increasing numbers employed in routine, low-paid and low-value jobs. This split reflects an increasingly polarized society. Yet the curriculum remains the same – preparing a workforce for work that no longer exists and ignoring the skills and qualities that are needed to participate in the creation of national and personal wealth.

Hutton's (1996) analysis of the British economy in 1995 highlights the trends that are still being lived through by many:

> The British credit boom generated the biggest rise in personal debt of any industrialized country in this period. The growth in inequality has been the fastest of any advanced state. The drop in the relative importance of manufacturing has been the most marked. The economy has been more volatile. The privatization programme was among the most aggressive of any advanced state. The attack on the welfare system has been more comprehensive. The deregulation of the financial system was the most complete; the assault on labour market regulation the most all-encompassing. The cuts in the top rate of tax were the largest. The market principle has been driven deeper into society. No Western industrialized country in the twentieth century has been subjected to such fast and extensive marketization. (page 18)

For many, these economic changes have brought about a contradictory state of affairs. The poor are less poor, in relative terms, and we have redefined the basics of life; the vast majority of households now have kitchen 'white goods' as a norm, while telephones and televisions are basics. Yet this has resulted in massive levels of debt, the longest working hours in Europe and either a resignation to unsatisfying work or a desire to escape to create a new life.

The death sentence of work in the mines has been replaced by the tedium of the call centre. The traditional hard-earned skills of the manufacturing industry have been replaced by short-term skills for short-term employment. The concept of a career has been replaced by serial employment, which makes new types of demands in terms of adaptability, resilience and flexibility. Personalization offers the possibility of helping individuals to develop the capacity to live and flourish in such a world and to be able to respond to the questions set by Sachs (2003):

> Of any economic system we must ask: Does it enhance human dignity? Does it create self-respect? Does it encourage creativity? Does it allow everyone to participate in the material blessing of this created world? Does it sustain a climate of equal regard – for employees as well as employers, the poor no less than the rich? Does it protect the vulnerable and help those in need to escape the trap of need? Does it ensure that no one lacks the means for a dignified existence? Do those who succeed share their blessings with those who have less? Does the economic system strengthen the bonds of human solidarity? (page 89)

The fragile world

Education is fundamentally about preparation for the future; learning is about the ability to respond to a rapidly changing environment. The world in which today's young people will live will be socially complex, environmentally challenging, technologically sophisticated and increasingly fragile. Consider the following observations about the natural world and the impact of global warming:

- It was thought that the snow on Mt Kilimanjaro would disappear by 2020 – in fact it had disappeared in 2005.

- The National Trust in England is working on a new planting scheme for its gardens in southern England – within 30 years it may not be possible to grow a traditional English garden.

- By 2050, on current predictions, the Arctic ice cap will disappear in the summer with potentially disastrous effects for sea levels around the world.

- The government of Vanuatu in the South Pacific is actively planning for the time when most of its islands will be rendered uninhabitable by rising sea levels.

- Winter temperatures in Alaska have risen by, on average, six degrees centigrade – spring now arrives a week earlier than in the 1920s. The permafrost is thawing.

- Ten of the past 14 years have been the world's hottest ever recorded.

- Glaciers in the European Alps halved in mass between 1850 and 1990 – at this rate they will be a quarter of their original size by 2025.

And so on.

If we are to avoid a global catastrophe then we may need to move from teaching about the environment to educating a generation that is capable of understanding and acting on the issues. As Lynas (2004) puts it:

> Don't leave climate change to the experts. When I began to get interested and campaign on this issue, I did so without having any formal scientific training, and was continually worried about being too ignorant to speak out. But climate change is a very simple issue, and everyone needs to get involved in combating it. (page 294)

> And this reality has no time at all for concerns about the wider impacts of the way we live: (page 296)

> The only way that this mindset will ever change is if more and more people stand up and speak the truth. It's a difficult truth, and an unpleasant one: that the world is facing climatic catastrophe, and we all have to change the way we live. (page 296)

Global warming *may* be the result of industrialization – notably mass production and the factory system. It may be that we find it so hard to challenge because our education system is still rooted in that factory system – an inability to accept personal responsibility and to understand and so personalize the issues.

This is also true of an increasingly complex political world in which the (retrospective) simplicity of the Cold War has been replaced by the uncertainty and ambiguity of international terrorism, ethnic wars, struggles for economic dominance and the never-ending need for one nation to impose its politics, values and ideology on another. We have come a very long way from the mass suicide of nationalistic pride of the First World War, but we need individuals who can think, judge, analyse and adjudicate more than ever before.

Chapter 3

Understanding learning

John West-Burnham

ny discussion about the nature of learning in the future risks indulging in false optimism – seeking to describe a Shangri-la. This is not the purpose of this discussion; rather it is to try to identify current knowledge and trends and extrapolate from them what our emerging understanding might lead to. We create the future; the decisions that we take now will determine the nature of schooling, educating and learning in the future. There can be little doubt that the past decade has seen an explosion of interest in the notion of learning. The historically dominant paradigm of learning as the product of teaching is being replaced by a recognition that teaching is a necessary but not sufficient condition for learning. This is being reflected in many ways in educational practice, not least in the Ofsted Framework, which has now separated teaching and learning as significant variables in assessing the effectiveness of classroom practice.

This discussion will focus on four areas where our understanding of the learning process is developing rapidly:

- learning as a process
- the science of learning
- learning as a social relationship
- intelligence and learning.

Each of these will be explored in turn and tentative conclusions drawn about their implications for educational practice. However, at the outset, it is necessary to explore exactly what is meant by learning. The term is ambiguous and used to describe a wide range of cognitive phenomena. If we are to understand the personalization of learning then we need to have an intellectually coherent model of what learning might be, as shown in Figure 3.1.

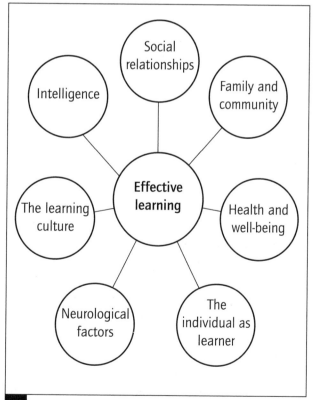

Figure 3.1 The variables influencing effective learning

Each component of Figure 3.1 is dealt with in detail in this chapter. What follows is a summary of the essential characteristics of each component of the diagram.

Effective learning is most likely to occur when:

- There are high-quality social relationships characterized by emotional intelligence, interdependence and high trust.

- The learner lives in an effective family and community in which there are shared values, high aspirations and economic security.

- The learner enjoys physical, psychological and emotional well-being underpinned by a suitable diet, and appropriate amounts of sleep and exercise.

- The learner understands him/herself as a learner, in other words is aware of his/her distinctive profile as a learner and is able to engage in meta-cognitive activities.

- There is awareness of the need to maximize neurological effectiveness – largely by optimizing the other variables.

- School, community and family focus on the social aspects of learning, for example ensuring access to mentoring and working in effective groups.

- There is a strategy to enhance the potential of each person in terms of a model of intelligence that reflects a scientific and humanistic approach rather than social prejudice.

All learning requires the positive interaction of a range of complex variables; the possibility of effective learning taking place depends on optimizing the variables. The variables are shown in Figure 3.1, but it is essential to stress that the relative significance of each will vary from individual to individual. The diagram creates an artificial sense of balance and equity.

The figure represents the strongest case for personalizing learning. It is only by understanding the relative significance of each factor for any one individual that it becomes possible to be confident about his/her potential and capacity to learn.

Learning as a process

For many educators the concept of learning is implicit and assumed. In some usages it implies what the learner does in response to teaching: 'If you don't pay attention to me you won't learn this.' A common usage equates learning with memorization: 'I want you to learn this for a test tomorrow.' The paucity of our understanding of learning is often reflected in the lack of any shared or common agreement between teachers, let alone learners, as to what the process actually involves. Although the situation is now changing, many schools do not have a shared vocabulary as to what constitutes learning – it is usually judged as a product rather than a process – 'I have learned this.' What 'learning this' actually involves is elusive and not codified. There is little doubt that this is, to a significant extent, the result of a curriculum that is focused on information transfer and the means of assessment that value the 'correct' answer. Most national schooling systems focus on this narrow, instrumental and reductionist view of learning and this is reinforced by prevailing models of accountability, which value outcomes that allow for generic comparability rather than individual capability.

What follows is an attempt to develop a model of learning that provides the basis for meaningful dialogue about the learning process and its related outcomes.

	Shallow: what?	Deep: how?	Profound: why?
Means	Memorization	Reflection	Intuition
Outcomes	Information	Knowledge	Wisdom
Evidence	Replication	Understanding	Meaning
Motivation	Extrinsic	Intrinsic	Moral
Attitudes	Compliance	Interpretation	Challenge
Relationships	Dependence	Independence	Interdependence
	(Single-loop learning)	(Double-loop learning)	(Triple-loop learning)

Figure 3.2 Modes of learning

It is important to stress at the outset that this model is not intended to be hierarchical; it is rather descriptive of the characteristics of different modes of learning. In some contexts shallow learning is entirely appropriate – my knowledge of how my car's engine works is shallow, but I hope that the mechanic's knowledge is deep if not profound. Equally, it is important not to impose academic values on this model; profound learning is about the more arcane branches of philosophy, but it is also about the qualities of a counsellor, the skills of a joiner and the moral insights of a child.

In many important respects, shallow learning is synonymous with the prevailing patterns of schooling – it is based on the memorization and replication of information. While it does not preclude deep and profound learning, schooling does limit and inhibit the potential to move beyond the shallow. Shallow learning has been adequate for a world that operated on high levels of compliance and dependence in the workplace and society. If it is true that the world is becoming a far more complex place, then it may be that the dominant mode of learning will have to change. Shallow learning may have been an acceptable foundation for life in a relatively simple world with fewer choices and greater hegemony, but it is clearly inadequate in a world of complex choices and limited consensus. A simple illustration of this is the present place of sex education in the curriculum. It is taught as a subject but it does not really seem to impact on behaviour – the UK has the highest level of teenage pregnancy, abortion and sexually transmitted diseases in Western Europe. Surely, the basis for sex education has to be the creation of understanding and the confidence that comes with personal wisdom.

We live in an age of information: more data are easily available to us than ever before – some of it is widely and openly available; some of it is specialized and arcane. In fact, the more arcane information is the more we esteem it. This perhaps explains the popularity and credibility attached to television quiz shows – on *Who Wants to be a Millionaire?* the more arcane the information the higher the reward. *University Challenge* is perceived to be serious because most of the information is highly esoteric, but, in essence, both of these programmes are just extensions of the pub quiz. Neither seeks explanation, demonstration or debate – only the replication of the right answer.

The emphasis on the 'right answer' inevitably produces a state of compliance and dependence. If a student wishes to be successful then he/she must produce the right answer, in other words comply with the teacher's view of what is correct – this inevitably leads to dependency on the teacher, which means that the student will predictably be motivated by external factors. Extrinsic motivation is the weakest and most fragile type of motivation and, crucially, it denies the autonomy of the individual.

Shallow learning is the basis of teaching and assessment in most education systems – even where there is evidence of personal understanding this will often only be replication of the teacher's understanding. A traditional curriculum will be a prescription of information, and assessment will be geared to the amount of information that can be accurately replicated. Shallow learning is essentially binary, right or wrong, but there is no guarantee that providing the right answer will enable usage of that information – a GCSE in German is no guarantee of being able to hold even a simple conversation in German; a GCSE in mathematics does not guarantee comfort in using mathematical procedures in daily life. Shallow learning, by definition, has a very short half-life – it decays rapidly.

The implications of shallow learning go beyond the individual. In their study of organizational learning, Argyris and Schön (1974) point to a similar manifestation in how organizations work:

> *When the error detected and corrected permits the organization to carry on its present policies or achieves its present objectives, then that error-and-correction process is* single-loop *learning. Single-loop learning is like a thermostat that learns when it is too hot or too cold and turns the heat on or off. The thermostat can perform this task because it can receive information … and take corrective action.* (page 2)

Shallow learning is appropriate and valid in many contexts, but if the experience of school presents it as the primary and dominant learning experience then learners will always be stuck at the 'what?' stage and never learn for themselves the 'how?' or 'why?'. The personalization of shallow learning would undoubtedly lead to an improvement in performance and, as such, is valid, but it also needs to explore those dimensions of learning that allow us to be effective in dimensions of our lives.

Deep learning provides the means to move from the replication of information to the creation of knowledge. In this context, information is seen as public, generic and unmediated: knowledge is personal. The pivotal criterion for the creation of knowledge is the development of understanding. According to Perkins (1992):

> The person who understands is capable of 'going beyond the information given,' in Jerome Bruner's eloquent phrase. To understand understanding, we have to get clearer about the 'beyond possession.'
>
> So let us view understanding not as a state of possession but one of enablement. When we understand something, we not only possess certain information about it but are enabled to do certain things with that knowledge. (pages 76–77)

Perkins goes on to define the 'certain things' as explanation, exemplification, application, justification, comparison and contrast, contextualization and generalization. The ability to engage in any of these 'performances' is to demonstrate deep learning. For example, the ability to replicate a list of the causes of the First World War is useful but shallow. More important is the ability of an individual to explain, prioritize, analyse, rationalize and justify them – this should be the basis of personalizing learning. This approach moves the learner from compliance to the ability to interpret, from dependence to interdependent learning through debate, discussion, mentoring and the creation of the relationship that Steiner describes:

> ... a lust for knowledge, an ache for understanding is incised in the best of men and women. As is the calling of the teacher. There is no craft more privileged. To awaken in another human being powers, dreams beyond one's own; to induce in others a love for that which one loves; to make of one's inward present their future: this is a threefold adventure like no other. (Steiner, 2003: pages 183–184)

Deep learning is fundamentally concerned with the creation of knowledge, which the learner is able to relate to their own experience and use to understand new experiences and contexts. The deep learner is thus able to integrate theory and practice, to create holistic models and to distinguish between evidence and debate. Crucially, deep learners know how to create knowledge, they are reflective about *what* they learn and *how* they learn; it is double-loop learning that:

> ... occurs when error is detected and corrected in ways that involve the modification of an organization's underlying norms, policies and objectives. (Argyris and Schön, 1974: page 2)

Questioning the 'norms and policies' means that processes are as important as product or outcome. The processes associated with deep learning are discussed in detail in Chapters 4 and 6. For practical purposes, deep learning involves the movement into metacognition and this is the essence of personalization – the learner understands him/herself as a learner. Intrinsic motivation requires a sense of personal control and this requires the ability to assume responsibility for every aspect of learning.

Profound learning is what makes us a person, it gives us a sense of uniqueness and determines our ability to think and act for ourselves. Profound learning is the way in which we develop personal wisdom and meaning, which allows us to be creative, to make moral judgements, to be authentic human beings who are able to accept responsibility for our own destinies. It is about moving from the ability to recite the catechism to having a genuine sense of our own spirituality – from knowing the rules to having the confidence to apply them in new and complex situations. But it is also about the skill of the wood-turner, the compassion of the nurse, the empathy and understanding of the counsellor, the skills of the athlete – in fact anything that makes us distinctive human beings. Profound learning builds on shallow and deep learning and is the ultimate expression of personalization. This is triple-loop learning: engaging with fundamental assumptions about who we are and how we engage with the world.

The nature of learning in the future will be substantially determined by the shared perceptions of the purpose of learning. This in turn might best be expressed in terms of the needs of the learner; a focus on deep and profound learning would produce the following definition of the learner in the future:

The autonomous learner

The autonomous learner knows how to learn and has a disposition to do so. She can identify, on her own, and/or with others, a problem, analyse its components and then marshal the resources, human and non-human, to solve it.

She continuously questions herself and others as to whether she is employing the best methods. She can explain the processes of her learning and its outcomes to her peers and others, when such a demonstration is required. She is able to organize information and, through understanding, convert it into knowledge. She is sensitive to her personal portfolio of intelligences. She knows when it is best to work alone, and when in a team, and knows how to contribute to and gain from teamwork. She sustains a sharp curiosity and takes infinite pains in all she does.

Above all, she has that security in self, built through a wide and deep set of relationships and through her own feelings of worth fostered in part by others, to be at ease with doubt, and to welcome questioning and probing of all aspects of her knowledge. (This definition was developed by Christopher Bowring-Carr.)

Deep and profound learning occur in every classroom and school every day, but often this is in spite of the prevailing curriculum, patterns of assessment and modes of teaching. The issue is to optimize the likelihood of deep and profound learning being available to all as an entitlement and as the core purpose of the school. Deep learning occurs when understanding is achieved, and this is fundamental to any aspect of life – driving a car, medical research, writing poetry, preparing a meal, becoming a moral person – and all require personal understanding to ensure success and personal authenticity. The rest of this discussion focuses on how current research might inform practice in schools in order to maximize the possibility of deep and profound learning.

The science of learning

There is probably not a science of learning at present. There is no synthesis available of the wide range of scientific research that may impinge on our understanding of the learning process. Research into genetics, neurological functioning and cognitive psychology do seem to point to the possibility of increased empirical knowledge about how we learn. However, it would be premature to claim that there is a holistic theory of learning in the offing. It is equally important to view with caution claims made on the basis of research which was never intended to inform learning and teaching in schools. And then there are the panaceas promoted as the basis of limited scientific research but with no claim to universifiability – open access to water, Brain Gym® or playing Mozart are not harmful, they *may* indeed be helpful but they are not based on scientific research. Inevitably, the picture is much more complicated in that our behaviour, and therefore our capacity to learn, is the result of a complex series of permutations and interactions in the brain, which are, in turn, the result of our learned experiences.

> *This tight orchestration of thought and feeling is made possible by what amounts to a superhighway in the brain, a bundle of neurons connecting the prefrontal lobes, behind the forehead – the brain's executive decision-making center – with an area deep in the brain that harbors our emotions.* (Goleman, 1996: page 24)

As our understanding of this relationship grows so do the implications for the management of the learning process and Pinker (2002: page 40) argues that it is possible to identify three interacting components of the brain:

- It has distinct interaction processing systems for 'learning skills, controlling the body, remembering facts, holding information temporarily, and storing and executing rules'.

- Second, there are mental faculties 'dedicated to different kinds of content, such as language, number, space, tools, and living things'.

- Third, there are the systems for motivation and emotion, the 'affect programs'.

Pinker (2002) concludes:

> *Behaviour is not just emitted or elicited, nor does it come directly out of culture or society. It comes from an internal struggle among mental modules with differing agendas and goals.* (page 40)

From this perspective, brain functioning, and therefore learning, can be seen as a complex interplay between information processing, mental faculties and the affect programmes. These factors, what Pinker calls 'combinatorial software', are the essence of our capacity to learn and use that learning. Our knowledge of these three elements is limited; even more uncertain is how they interact and how the multiple permutations they offer might be better understood and managed. What is clear, and available, is the potential for learners to develop and enhance each of these elements and so enrich their 'combinatorial' capacity.

Hard scientific data about learning are very elusive but there are significant developments, which may lead to profound changes in the conceptual framework, that inform our thinking about the nature of learning. The findings of the Human Genome Project have led to equal outbursts of optimism and pessimism about the future of the human race. For some there is hope that genetic engineering will remove most of the ills that assail humanity, and the positive attributes will be enhanced and extended. This prospect has led others to reinforce the centrality of human experience as the key determinant of our lives, in other words we come into the world as blank slates. Educational theory and practice have been very largely dominated by a view of the world that, according to Pinker (2002),

> ... *divides matter from mind, the material from the spiritual, the physical from the mental, biology from culture, nature from society, and science from the social sciences* ... (page 31)

Not surprisingly, educationalists have believed and created an education system around the belief that the schooling process is the means by which the tabula rasa or blank slate is filled. As Pinker caricatures it, 'children come to school empty and have knowledge deposited in them' (page 222). For Pinker:

> *Education is neither writing on a blank slate nor allowing the child's nobility to come into flower. Rather, education is a technology that tries to make up for what the human mind is innately bad at.* (page 222)

> *Our genetic and evolutionary inheritance means that we have a predisposition to speak; we do not have such a predisposition to write. Education is a process of compensating for gaps in our biological inheritance and adapting natural predispositions 'to master problems for which they were not designed'.* (page 223)

> *And this offers priorities for educational policy: to provide students with the cognitive tools that are most important for grasping the modern world and that are most unlike the cognitive tools they are born with.* (page 235)

This is an argument for both a better understanding of the impact of our genetic inheritance and recognition that the blank slate and genetic determinism arguments are both wrong.

Our capacity to learn is the result of complex interactions at the most fundamental level of what makes us human. The most powerful expression of this interaction is our neurological functioning. The brain is the most powerful example of the interaction between our genetic make-up and the environment in which we live. The starting point for this discussion has to be a very simple but highly contentious proposition – learning is a physical process. There is no 'ghost in the machine'.

> *So everything we think and feel can ultimately be boiled down to this alternating sequence of electrical and chemical events. The electrical signal arriving along the axon is converted into a chemical signal that carries it across the physical barrier, the synapse, between the neurons.* (Greenfield, 2000: page 39)

Although it would be wrong to claim any sort of direct correlation between neurological research and classroom practice, it is worth noting the range of neurological functions that have a demonstrable impact on all learning processes:

- attention span and concentration

- threat and stress

- motivation

- the emotions

- memory

- neural processing.

Jensen (1998) demonstrates the complexity and difficulties in relating our intentions, in supporting the learning of others, with what we know about how the brain functions:

> *In summary, we know the ingredients, but not the recipe. The ability to make meaningful patterns and use context seems to be activating frontal lobes. The ability to engage relevance uses our past experiences, and that domain is our temporal lobes. Meaning-making from emotional activation is more likely originating in the mid-brain's reward circuit. Thalamus, amygdala, and even lower parietal areas are involved. Meaning-making is complex. Any one of the three ingredients can trigger it, but none is guaranteed. This suggests we ought to evoke all of them in our general practices.* (page 96)

Carter (1998) provides a similar link between our understanding of learning and brain activity:

> *The nuts and bolts of thinking – holding ideas in mind and manipulating them – take place in a region of cortex on the dorsolateral (upper side) prefrontal cortex. This is also the location of the closely related activity called working memory. Planning takes place in this area, and it is here that choices are made between various possible actions. Some studies suggest that each type of information has its own special temporary storage niche. An area in the upper reaches of the right hemisphere prefrontal lobe, for example, has been found to light up when a person holds information about objects that are temporarily out of sight. Another spot nearby seems to hold the memory of how many times you have done a thing before. This may be part of a sort of metamemory – the ability to 'know what you know' and to recognize when a particular activity has been 'done to death' – both of which are skills that often seem to be missing in people with frontal lobe damage.* (page 195)

Our capacity to learn is the result of an incredibly complex equation of which neural processing is only a part. It would be difficult to produce a list of all the factors influencing learning without listing everything that informs who we are as people. However, as our knowledge of neurological functioning improves it might be increasingly possible to help individuals understand the optimal circumstances that inform their potential to learn. Any summary of these issues is bound to be a parody, but it is possible to identify a range of implications for educators about research into the brain:

- There is a need for a much greater understanding of the development of the brain, and learning potential, in the early years.

- Effective learning is an individual phenomenon – every brain is unique – and there needs to be much more explicit recognition of the individual disposition to learn.

- Teaching needs to pay more attention to the variable that influences engagement with learning, for example choice of learning activities, time on task, appropriate levels of challenge, development of cognitive skills and strategies, especially memory.

- The psychological aspects of learning need greater recognition – even though the effects may be long term. Health is a vital component of effective brain functioning.

- Human relationships, especially in the family, have a profound impact on learning capacity. Effective neurological functioning is significantly determined by the emotional state of the learner.

Learning as a social relationship

The increasing recognition of the importance of emotional intelligence in all aspects of human collaboration is firmly rooted in neurological science. The core proposition is very simple – our emotional responses to the world are so powerful that they can overwhelm most cognitive processes. For Greenfield (2000):

> *The question of emotions is one of the most important that a brain scientist, or indeed anyone, can explore. We are guided and controlled by our emotions. They shape our lives as we attempt to maximize some, such as happiness, and obliterate others, such as fear.* (page 107)

Simplistic thinking in this area sees the brain as a battleground between the emotions and reason, between EQ (emotional quotient) and IQ (intelligence quotient). This may be the very heart of learning in the future and learning for the future – developing strategies to enhance the potential and capacity of every person: replacing knowing 'what?' to knowing 'how?'. The work of Gardner and others on multiple intelligences, and Goleman and others on emotional intelligence, demonstrate the potential for building the capacity to learn on the basis of focused interventions.

Gardner (1999b: page 81) identifies seven implications for educators growing out of brain and mind research:

1. The tremendous importance of early experience.

2. The imperative 'use it or lose it'.

3. The flexibility of the early nervous system.

4. The importance of action and activity.

5. The specificity of human abilities and talents.

6. The possible organizing role played in early childhood by music.

7. The crucial role played by emotional coding.

Each of these is an intervention – the result of learning and teaching strategies, which have the potential to develop (nature via nurture!) all aspects of human potential. The development of appropriate learning strategies will create richer, stronger and more resilient networks of neurons, which, with repetition, will become the brain's default option – our automatic and spontaneous response. Our emotions inform our learning at the neural, personal and interpersonal levels. Developing our interpersonal relationships and capacity to understand our emotional selves has a direct impact on our neural functioning. The health of the neural network is a product of that of the social network and vice versa.

Perhaps the most important component of the social network is the family. In Gardner's list, above, most of the factors can be directly associated with the quality of family life. In his major review of the impact of family life on a child's educational achievement, Desforges (2003) concludes:

> *Research also establishes that parental involvement has a significant effect on children's achievement and adjustment even after all other factors (such as social class, maternal education and poverty) have been taken out of the equation between children's aptitudes and their achievement. Differences in parental involvement have a much bigger impact on achievement than differences associated with the effects of school in the primary age range. Parental involvement continues to have a significant effect through the age range although the impact for older children becomes more evident in staying on rates and educational aspirations than as measured achievement.* (page 86)

and

> *What parents do with their children at home through the age range is much more significant than any other factor open to educational influence.* (page 91)

High-quality social relationships in the family have a direct impact upon the development of an individual as a learner. It would therefore seem appropriate to argue that personalization should start with the child in the family rather than the pupil in the classroom.

Effective family life is made up of a complex network of relationships that, depending on the size of the family, will usually involve sophisticated interactions between two, three or four people. There is powerful research evidence to suggest that this provides the model for the most powerful learning. Bloom (1984) demonstrated that tutoring (one-to-one teaching/ mentoring/coaching) is the single most powerful learning relationship. Examining the differences between a class of 30 and the impact of tutoring he found that in terms of both learning and cognitive development in higher mental processes, tutoring improved performance by two standard deviations (2σ) beyond the level of achievement in conventional classrooms.

This provides powerful empirical confirmation of Vygotsky's notion of the Zone of Proximal Development and Bruner's theory of scaffolding which, according to Mercer (2004):

> *… represents both teacher and learner as active participants in the construction of knowledge.*

> *The essence of the concept of scaffolding as used by Bruner is the sensitive, supportive intervention by a teacher in the progress of a learner who is actively involved in some specific task, but who is not quite able to manage the task alone.* (page 74)

Most parents will recognize this relationship; virtually all of us will have experienced a learning relationship with another person that has moved us beyond what we might have achieved on our own – learning to drive, swim, tell the time, ride a bicycle, play a musical instrument or talk. The most powerful learning relationship in our lives is the one-to-one with a person who we trust, who has the skills to take us forward, and with whom the emotional relationship develops as the learning relationship grows and matures. Edgar (2001) provides a powerful vindication of the role of the family:

> *… the family, in whatever form, is the foundation for every human child's human capital; it is the crucible of competence. It is also the starting point for every child's networks, its connections with the wider world, its sense of trust of and*

reciprocal obligations towards 'strangers' in the society as a whole. Married or not, single parent or two, first family or step, based on blood ties, adoption or simply deep friendship, families are the key mediation point between individual and society, the private self and the public self as employee, voter or community group member. (page 31)

Any model of personalization has to be based on the individual child in the family setting.

However, it is important to recognize that personalizing learning is not about individualization. Much of human life is rooted in social interaction, largely in groups of varying sizes. The ability to work and learn in groups and teams is as much a part of personalization as the ability to work alone or with a mentor. In Chapter 9, Hazel Pulley, headteacher of Caldecote Primary School, Leicester, describes her school's strategy to build effective relationships to support learning. Her account identifies a number of significant factors in creating a climate and culture for learning:

- the development of shared values;
- working through agreed protocols;
- developing metacognitive understanding through the use of relationships;
- providing ongoing support, development and training;
- celebrating success.

Intelligence and learning

The debate around the nature of intelligence is central to any view of learning in the future. Most education systems are still dominated by four fundamental assumptions about intelligence:

- intelligence is expressed through logical and reasoning abilities;
- those abilities can be measured quantitatively;
- such measures are predictive;
- intelligence is fixed for life.

These assumptions have led to patterns of schooling, assessment, the nature of the curriculum, models of accountability and dominant modes of teaching. A key influence in the UK is Cyril Burt who argues that intelligence is 80 per cent genetic in origin – which might explain the confidence in predestination implicit in many education systems. However, according to Ridley (2003) reviewing studies of twins:

IQ is approximately 50 per cent 'additively genetic', 25 per cent influenced by the shared environment and 25 per cent influenced by factors unique to the individual. (page 90)

Ridley points to two other crucial findings; first, living in poverty has a profound impact on IQ – environment outweighs genetics. Second, ageing reduces the effect of family environment on IQ and genetic factors become more significant. If these points are accepted then many of the fundamental assumptions underpinning schooling are called into question.

Schooling fails to come to terms with environmental issues and what we are learning about the influence of genetics. The essential model of schooling is a reflection of theoretical assumptions; if they change, then the model of schooling has to change. To build an educational system around IQ, which is so culturally and chronologically specific, is to deny the full human potential of an individual.

> *I view giftedness as being of multiple kinds, as would be retardation. Componential, experimental and contextual strengths and weaknesses can all lead to different patterns of giftedness or retardation, and hence, for me, giftedness and retardation are in no way unitary phenomena.* (Sternberg, 1990: page 299)

Sternberg's view has, of course, much in common with Gardner's view of multiple intelligences: both offer a response to the potentially inhibiting model based around IQ. If our understanding of intelligence moves from a unitary to a federal model then a range of assumptions about the nature of the curriculum, the role of the teacher, the patterns of assessment and accreditation are all called into question. Gardner shows just how fundamental the challenge is:

> *For those who believe that human beings have a desire to explore and to understand the most fundamental questions of existence, and that curricula ought to be organized around the teaching of these epistemological concerns – familiarity, the true, the beautiful and the good.* (1999b: page 226)

The response to this challenge lies in what Gardner characterizes as 'literacy skills, disciplinary skills and the possibility of multidisciplinary or interdisciplinary approaches' (Gardner, 1999b). A further challenge to the historical model of intelligence is the recognition that intelligence is, partly, a social construct based on interactions.

> *… I want to capture the important fact that intelligence, which comes to life during human activities, may be crafted. There are both social and material dimensions of this distribution.* (Pea, 1997: page 50)

Intelligence is constructed socially through relationships and interactions; the material dimension is in response to the environment and artefacts. Intelligence can thus be said to be constructed; in fact intelligence can be learned and can be taught, if we change the definition of intelligence. We have changed our definitions of democracy, family and culture; so it may now be time to develop a new understanding and shared usage around the concept of intelligence.

Csikszentmihalyi (1997) offers a powerful model to help us place the debate about intelligence in context:

> *Generally, when the issue of thinking comes up, most people assume it must have to do with intelligence. They are interested in individual differences in thinking, such as: 'What's my IQ?' or: 'He is a genius in math.' Intelligence refers to a variety of mental processes; for instance, how easily one can represent and manipulate quantities in the mind, or how sensitive one is to information indexed in words. But as Howard Gardner has shown, it is possible to extend the concept of intelligence to include the ability to differentiate and to use all kinds of information, including muscle sensations, sounds, feelings, and visual shapes.* (page 27)

For Csikszentmihalyi the central feature of effective learning is flow:

> *These exceptional moments are what I have called* flow *experiences. The metaphor of 'flow' is one that many people have used to describe the sense of effortless action they feel in moments that stand out as the best in their lives. Athletes refer to it as 'being in the zartists and musicians as aesthetic rapture. Athletes, mystics, and artists do very different things when they reach flow, yet their descriptions of the experience are remarkably similar.* (page 29)

Csikszentmihalyi goes on to identify the factors that are most likely to lead to flow:

- A clear set of outcomes that require a proactive response.

- Immediate feedback that provides a clear indication of progress.

- A challenge that is attainable but stretching.

- Skills that are appropriate to the challenge.

When all of these elements are in place then we are most likely to experience meaningful success that reinforces our desire to learn.

> *Thus the flow experience acts as a magnet for learning – that is, for developing new levels of challenges and skills. In an ideal situation, a person would be constantly growing while enjoying whatever he or she did.* (Csikszentmihalyi, 1997: page 33)

Learning for the future

Based on what has been discussed in this chapter, it is possible to begin to draw some tentative conclusions about what actions might be taken now in order to create a model of learning in the future and learning for the future. The fundamental issue is to create an effective dialogue between professional educators and those carrying out research into all branches of neuroscience and cognitive development. At present, educationalists are working by inference and innuendo, feeding off the crumbs when they should be sitting at the table as equal participants. There is an obvious need for a radical change in the perception as to what constitutes professional knowledge and the creation of new communities of practice centred on the application of scientific research to professional practice in schools. The implications of such a partnership might include:

- A focus on the need to design learning programmes around the individual as a unique learner rather than as a member of a class. This implies much more than the diagnosis of learning styles, rather a detailed profile of all the variables that are likely to have an impact on the individual's ability to learn. In medical terms, moving from an X-ray to a full body scan.

- A recognition of the impact of the social environment as a crucial determinant of educational success. The significant improvements in public health in the nineteenth century were partly the result of improvements in medical practice but were substantially the result of improvements in the basic infrastructure: clean water and sewers. Real improvement in the learning of all will only come when the issues of social equity are addressed.

- The introduction of programmes to enhance cognitive ability – what might be called the 'cognitive curriculum' – that might take the form of a range of interventions to enhance the skills that Gardner outlines above. The content-based curriculum would become the vehicle for the cognitive curriculum rather than, as at present, an end in itself.

- As part of the cognitive curriculum, far greater emphasis needs to be placed on the cultivation of personal and social skills, the concept of emotional intelligence. This has implications for effective learning, the development of social skills, employability and, crucially, the social expression of moral principles.

- A review of our understanding of assessment, both what is assessed and how it is assessed, which, in essence, is moving from summative to formative and from assessment of learning to assessment for learning.

- A radical rethinking of the role of the teacher, moving from the manager of information to the facilitator of the learning of the individual. Central to this change is the development of the role of the educator as coach through the pivotal relationship in the facilitation of learning.

- A focus on the development of ICT to support the learning process, especially the development of cognitive skills such as memorization, problem solving, analysis and information management.

Fundamental to all of these points is an emphasis on the early years of learning; neurologically, socially and morally. Investment in the early years seems to be the one thing that is most likely to create a learning society through the development of personalized approaches.

Chapter 4

A new model of the curriculum

John West-Burnham

The concept of a curriculum has numerous interpretations; this book argues that a curriculum is much more than a tool to create useful citizens, employees or undergraduates. It must also be the means by which young people can start to find themselves, begin the process of discovering their potential, strive for an ethical awareness, and learn how to cope with the enormously complex and rapidly changing world in which they live. This chapter suggests that the curriculum, as currently conceived and implemented, is totally inadequate to that task of creating autonomous, educated individuals.

A curriculum is essentially a cultural artefact; it is an expression of historical imperatives, cultural norms, economic demands and social hegemony. Establishing a curriculum is a key political process because of its actual and symbolic power, and in many ways the development of a curriculum is an opportunity for a government to ensure the expression and reinforcement of its key ideology. Hence, in fascist states in the 1930s the curriculum was one of the most explicit manifestations of the prevailing political ideology. Equally, with the collapse of communism in the late twentieth century, the creation of a 'new' curriculum was a potent symbol of political and social change. A major element in the assimilation of the former East Germany into the united Germany was the introduction of new curriculum models and, crucially, consequent changes to pedagogy and school management. In the UK, the curriculum, once taken out of the 'secret garden', was seen to be in need of being made 'relevant'. The problem is that quite what sort of society is the template against which the relevance is to be judged has never been made clear and, in any case, changes as governments come and go.

Most curricula are products of the political process and are the direct manifestations of a prevailing ideology. As such, they are not necessarily anything to do with education per se but rather the replication and extension of the prevailing political orthodoxy. The curriculum is essentially a policy and therefore subject to the constraints of all policy making. Two of the most significant pragmatic constraints on policy making at government level are, first, that the primary purpose of political policy making is to retain power and secure the successful careers of politicians. This inevitably inhibits the potential for creative and lateral thinking. Second, policy making tends to be 'generational', that is, it takes a generation (say 25–30 years) for policy makers to catch up with social trends. Thus, in England, major reforms on social issues, such as homosexuality, abortion, divorce and the use of 'soft' drugs, have tended to consolidate changes in social behaviour and expectations that have long since become the prevailing orthodoxy. While politicians remain in control of the curriculum, it is highly unlikely that these two imperatives will change. However, what this chapter seeks to do is to argue for curriculum reform on the basis of educational and social reality rather than political imperatives.

The central hypothesis of this chapter is that the context of education has changed, and continues to change, so radically that the prevailing notion of what constitutes an appropriate curriculum is increasingly irrelevant and outmoded. The current situation in education is akin to generals fighting the last war, solicitors practising on the basis of the law that prevailed when they were trained, and doctors ignoring advances in medication and surgical techniques. Each of these would be seen as morally reprehensible and professionally culpable, yet in education we continue to use the pony express rather than the electric telegraph, let alone the internet, and X-rays rather than CAT (computerized axial tomography) scans.

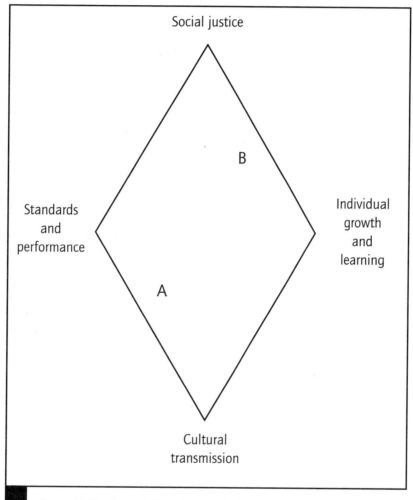

Figure 4.1 The forces influencing curriculum design

Any curriculum is a compromise – an attempt to reconcile a range of potentially conflicting imperatives. Figure 4.1 attempts to model one perspective on the various competing demands using the fundamental assumptions that determine curriculum design.

It could be argued that the current situation in many education systems would be located at point A on Figure 4.1, a balance between improving performance through a focus on standards and transmitting cultural values. This book is arguing that the curriculum should be located at point B and this theme is developed in detail throughout this chapter.

The remainder of this chapter is devoted to exploring the broad principles that might inform the development of a curriculum that is focused on personalizing learning. The discussion therefore is centred on the 'how?' of learning rather than the 'what?'. Three areas of the traditional curriculum are taken for granted in this discussion: literacy, numeracy and using ICT to support learning. This latter topic is explored in detail in Chapter 7.

Literacy is, of course, fundamental to any concept of education – it is the key component of any model of education, learning or a curriculum. It underpins every component of the discussion that follows – it serves as the basis for any understanding of the self, the development of the ability to think, to reflect on learning, and to learn with others, the family and the community. Literacy is also, of course, fundamental to numeracy and the effective use of ICT.

Although literacy, numeracy and the ability to use ICT are taken for granted in the majority of what constitutes a curriculum (subjects) and are ignored in this chapter, if personalization is taken to its logical possibilities then subjects become, at best, a means or a vehicle for learning. Shallow learning (see page 35) is expressed through a curriculum that requires the accumulation and replication of information. As we move into deep and profound learning, so the emphasis switches away from content to process with the learner exercising choice from the vast range of the canon of information and knowledge that constitutes our intellectual heritage. It is conceded that this represents a major heresy.

In England, the curriculum was originally largely determined by the Clarendon Commission, which reported in the 1860s. In order to restore confidence in England's public (private!) schools it laid down the components of the curriculum in terms of subjects. The basic list has remained unchanged for almost 140 years, apart from the introduction of business studies and ICT (as a subject) in the twentieth century and citizenship in the twenty-first century. The English National Curriculum has undergone significant changes in terms of emphasis and presentation but it remains focused on subjects. The teaching profession derives much of its identity and career structure from this focus on subjects and, of course, the secondary school day (and increasingly the primary-school experience) is defined in terms of subjects. The net result of this is the creation of information presented in undifferentiated ways. As Gardner (1999b) explains:

> In times past, schools have been uniform, in the sense that they taught the same materials in the same way to all students, and even assessed all students in the same ways. This procedure may have offered the illusion of fairness, but in my view it was not fair, except to those few blessed students strong in the linguistic and logical domains. If one seeks an education for all human beings, one that helps each achieve his or her potential, then the educational process needs to be conceived quite differently.
>
> In short, school must be individualized and personalized. (page 72)

The impact of ICT has the potential to create the situation where:

> All students may receive a curriculum tailored to their needs, learning style, pace and profile of mastery, and record of success with earlier material and lesson. Indeed, computer technology permits us to realize, for the first time, progressive, educational ideas of 'personalization' and 'active, hands-on learning' for students all over the world. (Gardner, 1999b: page 44)

It is perhaps the most powerful illustration of the strength of the silo mentality that ICT and citizenship became subjects rather than ways of learning and living. The reification of an area of human experience into a subject allows it to be controlled, measured, organized and delivered in a consistent manner. Without a parallel emphasis of equal status on how to learn, what to learn will always be dominant. Yet, if you explore the ultimate expression of reminiscence therapy, the website of Friends Reunited, the memories are of personalities and experiences – not subjects. Every educator understands the importance of the 'hidden' curriculum or extra-curricular activities, yet by definition these are marginalized and often sacrificed. The school play, the field trip, the expedition, the charity project are often pivotal experiences in school life; they form the enduring memories and may be more genuinely educative than hours of subject lessons.

For Freire (1998):

> Why not discuss with the students the concrete reality of their lives ... Why not establish an 'intimate' connection between knowledge considered basic to any school curriculum and knowledge that is the fruit of the lived experience of the students as individuals? A pragmatic reactionary educator would probably say that there is no connection between one thing and the other ... that the function of the school is to teach and transfer contents – packages – to the students, which, once learned, will operate automatically. (pages 36–37)

It might be helpful to see the personalization of learning as a relationship between content and process – rather like two strands of DNA. For this to be achieved a significant amount of reconceptualization will be required. The shift from the curriculum as content to the curriculum as process is a substantial one, but it is already under active development in Australia, notably Tasmania, Queensland and South Australia, and in the primary curriculum in Northern Ireland (see Chapter 13). In England the work of the Campaign for Learning and the Royal Society for the Arts' *Opening Minds* project provides a radical critique of the prevailing orthodoxies in England. What follows is an attempt to provide an outline for a model of the curriculum that will enable the personalization of learning. The model discussed below will be presented from three perspectives:

- purpose
- values
- processes.

It is not the intention of this section to present an alternative curriculum; rather to offer the additional components of any curriculum that are needed to secure personalization.

The component elements of the curriculum are presented as a series of understandings:

> To move toward enhanced understanding, one must again adopt both cognitive and cultural perspectives. One must identify those internal representations in need of alteration; construct cultural practices that confront, rather than overlook, the obstacles to deeper understanding; and devise measures to determine whether the 'corrective cognitive surgery' has been effective. (Gardner, 1999b, page 123)

To move personalization from the enhancement of good teaching to the genuine focus on the individual learner there are seven areas that need to be given equal status in any model of the curriculum:

- understanding self
- understanding relationships

- understanding thinking
- understanding learning
- understanding creativity
- understanding values
- understanding community.

Figure 4.2 demonstrates the possible interdependence of the historic model of the curriculum with the additional focus on personalizing learning – what links the two strands in the focus on the individual as a learner, balancing content and process.

Literacy	Self
Numeracy	Relationships
ICT	Thinking
Science	Learning
Arts	Creativity
Humanities	Values
Technology	Community

Figure 4.2 Content and process in personalizing learning

The purpose of the curriculum

Figure 4.1 demonstrates a range of possible options and priorities for a curriculum. Figure 4.2 demonstrates the factors that need to be balanced. For personalization to have sustainability it has to be seen as a core component of a curriculum rather than a vehicle for enhancing existing purposes; personalizing learning is an end, not a means. This leads to a definition of the purpose of the curriculum that might have the following components:

1. **The development of an educated person**

   This implies that we understand what we mean by education – our systems are very good at schooling but education is more elusive and intangible. The definitions of an educated person might include:

   - a sense of their own value as a human being;
   - an awareness of their cultural inheritance;
   - a sense of responsibility for their own destiny;
   - a recognition of their interdependence with others;
   - confidence in their own moral and spiritual values; building hope and optimism through a sense of personal uniqueness.

   Much of this is captured in the southern African concept of Ubuntu: 'A person is a person through other people.' It is very difficult to achieve a balance between stressing the importance of the individual without appearing to deny the importance of interpersonal, social, family and community relationships.

2. The development of the ability to lead a full and healthy life

This recognizes that the development of the individual is directly related to their well-being – expressed through physical, psychological and social health.

- Develop a holistic understanding of the factors that contribute to personal well being.

- Understand the personal strategies that support the development of a healthy lifestyle.

- Develop the capacity to make valid and appropriate personal choices.

- Understand the importance of personal happiness as the basis of growth and development.

3. The development of social awareness

Personalizing learning requires enhanced social awareness – learning is a social process and our development as social beings can best be seen as a series of learning relationships.

4. The development of moral confidence

Any view of an educated person must include the sense of a moral person. This is a highly contested area of any theory of the purpose of a curriculum. In the context of personalization the emphasis surely has to be on the ability to make morally appropriate decisions rather than being told what those decisions should be – hence the ideal of 'moral confidence' – and the ability of the individual to make valid choices.

It is too easy to teach moral precepts and test the ability of learners to replicate them – a classic example of shallow learning. What is surely required is personal understanding that informs behaviour in an authentic way. For example, teaching sexual morality does not seem to have much impact on the levels of teenage pregnancy, abortion and sexually transmitted diseases. The development of personal moral confidence is rooted in an explicit and coherent set of personal values which, in turn, are derived from ethical systems that are personally coherent and understood. This is a powerful exemplification of the curriculum as enabling personal growth rather than replicating the knowledge of others.

5. The development of the ability to learn

This is the pivotal issue in any debate about the development of the curriculum to support personalization. If personalization is to be more than enhancing effective teaching then the development of the individual as a learner has to be a central tenet. The full implications of this have been explored in Chapters 1 and 3, but it is worth summarizing the fundamental components of this aspect of the purpose of the curriculum, which should exist to:

- enable the learner to be confident in directing their own learning;
- support the learner in understanding how they learn;

- develop the capacity to think, create knowledge and personal understanding;

- provide skills and strategies to manage information, learn from experience and translate theory into practice;

- create a love of the learning process.

Values and the curriculum

If defining the purpose of a curriculum helps to set its direction and priorities then it is also necessary to define the values that should inform the nature of the curriculum experience. For personalization to become embedded there has to be an explicit statement of the values that will determine the culture, ethos and nature of the way in which educational organizations work. To sustain personalization, and to ensure that it informs every aspect of the educational experience, the following principles need to be in place:

- respect

- social integration

- resilience

- success

- creativity

- equity.

Respect: there has to be fundamental regard for, and commitment to, the integrity of the individual as a learner. This is rooted in the recognition of the uniqueness of each individual and their right to be a significant voice in shaping their personal destiny.

Social integration: personalization is not about individualism; a curriculum for personalization has to recognize the importance of social relationships in the learning of each individual. Such relationships have to be characterized by a sense of mutual regard, interdependence, trust and the ability to work and learn collaboratively.

Resilience: implies a commitment to building stamina, engagement and motivation that is intrinsic to the person rather than a response to extrinsic pressures. Personalization requires a high degree of self-management and the acceptance of personal responsibility for shaping one's destiny.

Success: personalized approaches to learning have to be rooted in high aspirations and expectations with a strong sense of the achievement of personal potential. This implies the design of learning activities and projects that allow for success.

Creativity: if personalization is to allow the full expression of personal potential then it has to foster individual creativity, innovation and enterprise. This means allowing for the possibility of multiple directions and many competing realities.

Equity: there is a danger that personalization might be seen as a charter to enhance the most gifted and able. A fundamental principle, therefore, has to be a commitment to parity of esteem and the validity of many different pathways to learning and achievement.

The curriculum as a process

What follows is a list of the skills, competencies, strategies and behaviours that we believe are necessary to consolidate the personalization of learning. Unless each learner has access to this repertoire he or she will be unable to develop his or her full potential as an autonomous and self-directed learner. The components of this section are presented alphabetically as there are numerous alternative permutations of these elements – all valid – that will be determined by the specific context in which they are applied. All of these factors are present in every learning situation from the early years to the University of the Third Age. The problem is that they are usually the resources of the teacher – not the learner.

Analysis and synthesis includes:

- classifying information according to explicit criteria;
- developing a conceptual framework appropriate to the data being considered;
- being able to justify the sorting and prioritizing of information;
- demonstrating the internal logic and coherence of the analysis;
- presenting an integrated and valid synthesis.

Applying learning includes:

- translating theory into practice;
- demonstrating understanding of the practical implications of knowledge;
- showing confidence in using knowledge in differing contexts;
- being able to revise understanding in response to experience.

Causality includes:

- showing understanding of the internal logic of an argument;
- understanding the principles of inductive and deductive reasoning;
- being able to demonstrate fallacies in arguments;
- recognizing the difference between positivist and naturalistic statements.

Choosing and prioritizing includes:

- developing criteria to justify decision making;
- being able to recognize, explain and defend criteria for prioritizing;
- recognizing the implications of choices and priorities.

Creativity and innovation includes:

- demonstrating the ability to think laterally;
- understanding the techniques and strategies that support creativity and innovation;
- understanding how social interaction can support creativity.

Critical thinking includes:

- evaluating information for appropriateness, accuracy, validity and authenticity;
- developing the confidence to challenge, question and interrogate sources of information;
- being comfortable with ambiguity and uncertainty;
- recognizing bias and prejudice;
- demonstrating appropriate scepticism and iconoclasm.

Demonstrating understanding includes:

- being able to: explain, exemplify, apply, justify, compare and contrast, contextualize and generalize (Perkins, 1992);
- having the confidence to present and defend an argument;
- being comfortable with a wide range of assessment strategies.

Design and planning includes:

- understanding the importance of procedures, processes and structures in managing a project;
- understanding the portfolio of investigative techniques;
- having the confidence to explore alternative approaches and modify strategies;
- being able to explain and justify the strategies adopted;
- reviewing the project and understanding the implications for future projects.

Managing information includes:

- understanding the range of types of information and alternative sources;
- being confident in the use of libraries, ICT and people in gathering data;
- being able to structure, collate and present information in appropriate formats;
- understanding conventions governing the use of information.

Memory includes:

- understanding the neurological basis of memory;
- using techniques to improve the retention of information.

Negotiating includes:

- understanding the social process involved in collaborative learning;
- using a range of strategies to ensure effective communication and interpersonal effectiveness;
- recognizing the importance of influencing skills to secure consensus;
- having the confidence to challenge and question.

Problem solving includes:

- being comfortable and confident when faced with challenges and problems;
- being able to diagnose the exact nature of a problem;
- being able to analyse the component parts of a problem;
- developing a range of options and evaluating their relevance;
- reviewing the effectiveness of the chosen strategy.

Review and reflection includes:

- understanding the importance of review and reflection in the learning process;
- being able to review a process and accept feedback;
- being open and honest about personal strengths and areas for development;
- understanding and monitoring the factors influencing personal performance and being able to take appropriate action;
- recognizing the importance of being as honest and objective as possible about self;
- being able to recognize and celebrate success as well as understand failure;
- understanding the factors and people contributing to success.

Self-management includes:

- having a realistic and evidence-based model of self as a learner;
- developing resilience, optimism and self-belief;
- having high personal aspirations and expectations;
- maintaining focus and being persistent;
- understanding self in relation to others;
- having a compelling personal vision, dream and awareness of 'who and what I want to be'.

The taxonomy above is essentially about empowerment – giving every learner the knowledge, skills and qualities to move from dependence to independence. Personalizing learning will only work if schools *actively* strive to enhance the capacity of young people to engage in the learning process as partners. For Sizer and Sizer (1999) it is a fundamental moral issue:

> *What the young people should not experience is sustained hypocrisy. The school which claims that 'everyone can be what he can be' but which demonstrably discriminates or silently tolerates discrimination imposed by higher authorities sends a devastating message: Do as I say but not as I do. No message is more corrosive, especially for teenagers.*
>
> *As soon as we honestly focus on the 'curriculum' provided by the school's daily functioning, we get into a nest of particulars. Morality is not 'achieved,' like the soccer trophies or the essay contest certificates which stuff the glass cases in the*

school's front hall. The state of a school's goodness is far more fluid. It depends on what each person brings into the community every year – indeed, every day. A school is prizeworthy if inside every single head – adult and child, producer and consumer – there is a clear reference to principle in every decision and a determination to do the best thing. (page 117)

Chapter 5

Learning styles

Max Coates

In the Department for Education and Skills (2004b) pamphlet, *A National Conversation about Personalised Learning*, it is perhaps surprising that learning styles do not feature. There is mention of skills sets, varying aptitudes and aspirations, diverse teaching strategies and actively developing the confidence of learners by engaging and stretching them. Despite not appearing in the credits, it is unlikely that any dialogue about personalizing learning will move very far without touching on learning styles.

Experience has produced an intuitive resonance among teachers about the concept of learning styles. Attempts to standardize the curriculum, pedagogy and appearance of children in schools have not contained the belief that individuals differ in the ways in which they learn. Even the post-war grammar schools were based upon an unshakeable belief that there were some who listened (auditory learners), those who were better with their hands (kinesthetic learners) and, of course, the few who had a predilection for art and were drawn towards bright colours, abstraction and, possibly, eccentric lifestyles (visual learners). Even within families, where the gene pool is inevitably more concentrated, discussions are as likely to focus on differences between their children as they are on their similarities.

The recognition and application of these different approaches to learning have not been systematic and universally applied within education. In 2003, straw polls among secondary teachers about learning styles suggest that less than ten per cent had heard of them in any formal sense. This was true even in schools that had received input from some of the 'learning spin doctors'. More recently, there has been a significant rise in awareness, though this does not seem to have been matched with a commensurate rise in understanding about what they are, what they do, and what teachers should do with them.

From the 1990s onwards, there has been an unjustified emphasis on the visual, auditory and kinesthetic (VAK) model. Indeed, the Department for Education and Skills' website (2004a) seems to commend this view, offering a case study on Broughton Hall School in Liverpool that categorizes pupils in this way and supplies each child with a card marked with a 'V', 'A' or 'K'. Many schools now require lessons to demonstrate these different facets as an indicator of effective teaching. There appears to be a growing perception that these operate like a modem and, if teachers can configure the one installed in each particular child, then they can be connected to the educational super-highway. If only the promotion of learning was this easy. Learning styles remain theoretical constructs and are often underscored with strong philosophical commitments by their protagonists. They are representations of reality in the same way that a map is a representation of a particular geographical area. It is important to remember the map is not the territory and few, if any, have broken a leg crossing a map.

What is a learning style?

Learning is a complex and creative process. It draws heavily on individual differences and personal dispositions.

 Our brain is a democracy of ten thousand million nerve cells yet it provides us with a unified experience.

(Eccles, 1996: page 37)

It is paradoxical that, learning, which is surely the core purpose of education, does not have a consensual definition. When we learn we engage with information. This is represented within the brain, then incorporated with existing knowledge and subsequently applied in a personalized and reconstructed version to new situations. The brain creates a construct of reality, which is highly edited. It also has a considerable capacity to fill in 'missing pieces' of information to try to achieve a coherent model. This is called nominalization and is the process that often generates examination howlers. Our learning is also enabled and constrained by the impact of emotions. Thinking is not a wholly rational process. Learners are often more disposed to accept information from those with whom they share rapport, and reject information from those with whom they do not engage in a constructive manner. Consider for a moment the subject choices made in school at different stages and how often these are made on the basis of interpersonal experiences.

A project undertaken for the Learning and Skills Research Council has investigated claims made for learning styles and has generated a database of nearly 850 references relating to 70 theories in this area (Coffield et al., 2004). Thirteen of these theories were chosen for closer scrutiny. They identified a spectrum of theories that ranged from the simple diagnostic approaches like VAK to much more complex theories that drew on personality theory, such as Jackson's learning styles profiler.

The protagonists of the different theories appear to present their particular view as definitive. It is more likely that, like the Indian fable of the blind men who tried to comprehend an elephant by touch who came to various and divergent conclusions, each has explored a particular aspect and offers a part and not the whole. The array of theories does not provide a range of alternatives. It is not about comparing like with like as, for example, making a choice between a Volkswagen and a Ford. It approximates more closely to the comparison of different parts of a holistic network. Using the transport illustration, it is analogous to comparing a car with a motorway or a traffic light with a roundabout. Conner and Hodgins (2000) have concluded that learning styles are drawn from three schools of thought that approach the analysis of learning from different standpoints; perceptual modality, information processing and personality patterns.

Perceptual modality is understood as biologically based reactions to the physical environment. It refers to the primary ways that our bodies take in information using the senses: especially auditory, visual and kinesthetic. Pause for a moment and consider experiencing an explosion.

The brain generates a representation. It could have been seen as a flash followed by flying debris; for others hearing a loud noise would predominate. For some, perhaps those who have experienced an explosion, smell and sensation might be more significant dimensions.

Some people tend to respond more to visual input, others to sound and yet others to movement. In terms of language the visual learner will utilize phrases such as 'I see what you mean' or 'I get the picture'; the auditory learner will refer to 'I hear what you are saying' or 'It sounds good to me'. The kinesthetic learner will refer to 'I feel this way' or 'I'm touched by what you are saying'. Other indicators can be tonality, speed of speaking or posture. Eye movements can also provide an analysis; the visual learner will tend to look upwards, the auditory learner will look forward and the kinesthetic learner will tend to look downwards.

This is not the whole story, as the information is then processed within the brain. Learning takes place when new knowledge is incorporated with existing knowledge. The 'information processing' phase will give significance to particular pieces of information and discard others. The brain frequently utilizes a reticular operating system that selects or identifies information which is held to be pertinent or significant and discards that which is not deemed to be relevant. However well matched teaching and learning styles may be, the incorporation of new knowledge in a cognitive pattern, as intended by the teacher, is not guaranteed. Consider, for example, research that has been undertaken into the speed of retrieval of information (Collins and Quillian, 1969). It was discovered that some simple factual questions can be answered more quickly than others. People were asked to respond to a series of statements as to whether these were true or false. Two of the statements were: 'A canary can fly' and 'A canary has skin'. The average response time for the first statement was 1.39 seconds while to the second it was 1.47 seconds. Suspending, for a moment, deep feelings that the researchers would benefit from getting out more, it does demonstrate that the manner in which the brain stores information is complex. In a computer the first information that goes in is stored in the first available space; later information is stored in the next available space; and so on.

These differential times recorded for responding to the statements suggest that information is stored in a much more organized way in the brain. It is not simply placed in a random location but arranged to form part of a concept. Consider for a moment the impact of a school day with perhaps between four to eight subject-related periods that follow on one from the other, separated with a brief break to top up sugar and cholesterol levels. This frenetic structure does not readily support the processing of information and can lead to a conceptual bleed between subject boundaries. The incoming information becomes detached from its core and incorporated with potentially unrelated material. The curriculum structures and concepts that teachers impose are not always self-evident to the learners.

Some of the analyses of learning style seem to throw light on what is taking place. Over 30 years ago Pask (1976) examined the teaching of keyboard skills and how students learned the locations of letters on a 'qwerty' typewriter. It was observed that some people worked with information by sorting it into chunks and then putting the whole lot together. Others seemed to assemble information by building it progressively, rather like a child building a tower from blocks. The assembling from chunks was termed a serialistic learning style, and the building up like the tower a holistic learning style. Their work was used by the Open University during the 1980s in psychology courses to illustrate cognitive differences and raise questions as to how teachers should present classroom-based material.

Some years later another analysis was developed by Anthony Gregorc (1982), who suggested a series of four 'thinking styles':

- concrete sequential
- concrete random
- abstract random
- abstract sequential.

Concrete sequential thinkers process information in an ordered linear manner. Detail is important and there is a ready recall of facts, formulae and rules. They often feel at ease learning in a 'hands-on manner'.

Concrete random thinkers are in many ways similar to concrete sequential thinkers. However, they do have a greater willingness to step outside the frame, experiment and take limited risk. In style they are often divergent, at ease with problem solving and willing to consider the perspective of others.

Abstract random thinkers favour reflection and are very much at ease with feelings and emotions. A structured environment is felt to be constraining and deadlines are not easily accommodated. Visual clues are often supportive of this style.

Abstract sequential thinkers are logical, rational and intellectual. Many of the great philosophers have displayed this thinking style. They thrive in the world of theory and the abstract. Reading is often a major resource and they have a tendency to isolate themselves.

In the 1980s, Dorset local education authority, in conjunction with British Petroleum, sponsored the exploration of this approach within their schools. They were, for the era, pushing at the boundaries of teaching and learning, in this area at least. They utilized Gregorc's thinking-style test which provided an analysis of an individual's thinking style. In 1987 this was used at a secondary deputy heads' conference. Of the 53 deputies present, 48 proved to be concrete sequential thinkers with the rest scattered among the other three categories. On reflection this was not surprising as the majority were timetablers, organizing aspects of schools into compartments and time frames. It does, however, raise the question as to whether this group of deputies was an appropriate pool from which to draw future heads. If headship is about anything it is about compromise, handling ambiguity and creativity, and, in particular, managing individuals who will not conform to a predetermined role. As an activity, headship is not tidy and precise and is more about process than completion. It is very much a quest for the rainbow's end.

There are some parallels between the work of Pask (1976), Scott (cited in Pask, 1976) and Gregorc (1982). All these pieces of research provide insights into how the brain deals with quantities of information. Gregorc's work, in particular, draws explicit links between his analysis to the operation of the brain in relation to the left and right halves of the cortex. The view is widely held that the two halves of the brain have different cognitive functions: these are summarized in Table 5.1.

Gregorc's work links the abstract dimension with the right hemisphere and the concrete with the left. It is argued that one half predominates in much the same way that people are right and left handed. The dominant side would, therefore, influence the processing style. This is often refered to as hemispheric dominance. For theorists like Gregorc, the idea of learning appears to be seen as a 'game of two halves'.

Table 5.1 Hemispheric dominance	
Left brain	**Right brain**
Language	Forms and patterns
Logic	Spatial manipulation
Mathematical formulae	Rhythm
Sequence	Musical appreciation
Linearity	Images and pictures
Phonetic reading	Tune of a song
Part to whole	Whole-language reader
Analysis	Imagination
Words of a song	Learns whole first, then parts
Unrelated factual information	Daydreaming and visioning

Conner and Hodgins (2000) suggest a third category of learning styles: personality patterns. It is argued that each of us has a preferred, largely consistent and distinct way of perceiving, organizing and retaining information. Kolb's learning styles inventory, Myers–Briggs Type Indicator (MBTI®) and Gardner's multiple intelligences seem to operate in this area. They relate to dimensions of personality, and it remains unclear as to how much a person's particular style relates to genetic predisposition or to formative learning experiences. Matt Ridley (2003) recognizes the importance of each of these strands, but also makes the case for the interplay of 'nature' and nurture' as being complementary and interacting dimensions of human behaviour. He quotes Jim Hightower, a Texan politician, as stating:

 There ain't nothing in the middle of the road but a yellow line and a dead armadillo. (page 3)

It is uncertain in what way this clarifies the tension but it seemed too good a quote to miss!

This third category would readily accommodate what is currently the most influential and possibly the most controversial of the learning style models: Howard Gardner's multiple intelligences. The core of Gardner's theory, first advanced in *Frames of Mind: The Theory of Multiple Intelligences* (1983), suggests that each individual has a complete range of intelligences, but a small number of individuals operate at an extended level. His work grew out of his personal reflections as to why he could remember music but failed to remember faces. In 1983 he defined intelligence as 'the ability to solve problems, or to create products that are valued within one or more cultural settings'. More recently he has extended the definition drawing from the vocabulary of psychology and biology. Intelligence is now understood as:

> … *a bio-psychological potential to process information that can be activated in a cultural setting to solve problems or create products that are of value in a culture.* (Gardner, 1999a: pages 33–34)

Gardner currently suggests the following categories of intelligences:

- logical – mathematical, deals with numbers and logic

- verbal/linguistic – linked mainly with words

- bodily–kinesthetic, deals with body movements and the handling of objects

- musical – the area of rhythm and melody

- visual/spatial – the dimension of pictures and images

- interpersonal – relates to understanding people and working with them

- intrapersonal – linked to personal reflection and understanding one's feelings

- naturalist – the classification and understanding of the phenomena of nature.

Gardner has considered adding a ninth intelligence, the existentialist or spiritual, which relates to the big questions of life. It would appear to come close to the concept of spiritual intelligence advanced by Zohar and Marshall (2000).

The significance of learning styles

If the medication we take was prescribed with the same level of evidence that underpins learning styles, it is unlikely that it would ever be taken. Every theory appears to have detractors. There is a great deal of passion surrounding the issue and there have even been threats of legal action when potential challenge to a particular stance has occurred. Gardner continues to be a target and multiple intelligences has been criticized on the basis of its research methodology (Ceci, 1990), its use of physiology (White, 1998) and on the essential definitions of the term 'intelligences' (Sternberg, 1999). In one sense Gardner's intention is to be provocative. He is quoted in Armstrong (2000):

> I'm deliberately being provocative. If I'd said that there are seven kinds of competencies, people would yawn and say 'Yeah, yeah'. But by calling them intelligences, I'm saying that we've tended to put on a pedestal one variety called intelligence, and there's actually a plurality of them, and some are things we've never thought about as being intelligence at all.

Perhaps the current significance of the work on learning styles is less about the impact on pedagogy and more about the impact on the beliefs that underpin the organization of schools and the practice of teaching. Education in the last century was dominated by the concept of intelligence. Derived from Alfred Binet's work in 1904 and popularized in Britain by Cyril Burt, this view of human intelligence had three cornerstones:

- that intelligence was significantly inherited

- that intelligence was largely fixed

- that there is a core cognitive process from which all abilities ultimately flow.

The legacy of this view lives on and many teachers continue to label children, believing that assessment reveals more about 'ceilings than floors'. Many teachers have beliefs that their students' potential is predetermined by innate ability (or its lack of) or by post code. Recent work in a secondary school in the south west of England has utilized the well established Keele attitudinal data to examine limits to student achievement. The work has suggested that the single biggest factor limiting this achievement has been teacher beliefs about their pupils' ability and attitude.

The research into learning styles has had a significant impact on challenging these views. It has stressed cognitive diversity. A one-size pedagogy does not fit all. If theorists and researchers like Gardner are correct, a monochrome pedagogical approach will not fit all the members of a given class of students. Indeed, consider for a moment the very term 'class' with its inherent categorizing of groups of students implicitly underscoring the belief in batch production.

The extensive range of learning-style constructs does not make the selection of appropriate strategies easy for the teacher. It does confirm, if only by sheer weight of numbers, that there are differences in the ways that individuals learn. A failure to engage with the provision of a range of strategies for learning limits the access to information and does not support cognition. The inevitable consequence can only be reduced achievement. For some students this will have profound impact upon their self-esteem and, in turn, lead to unconstructive behaviour patterns.

It would be facile to suggest that these issues have not been considered by many teachers. There are considerable numbers of examples where innovative work has been undertaken. At the end of this chapter is a brief case study that provides one such example. The change is not, however, universal. A MORI poll, undertaken in 2002, identified the two most common class-based practices in English secondary schools as being:

- copying from the textbook
- answering questions from the textbook.

Reference has already been made to the work of Coffield et al. (2004) in the area of learning styles. Their research provides an interesting analysis of the underpinning beliefs of the various authors and protagonists of these studies into the link between motivation and achievement. They have represented these views on a spectrum that reflects the associated views about the nature of these learning characteristics. For some, such as Gregorc (1999), and Dunn and Dunn (cited in Coffield et al., 2004), learning styles are viewed as largely fixed. Gardner is a little more flexible in his views. Other writers, such as Sternberg (1999), Kolb, and Pask and Vermunt (both cited in Coffield et al., 2004), consider these styles less fixed.

Applying learning styles to student learning

With the various writers taking up these foundational positions on the nature of learning styles and the nature of learners themselves, some reflection about the implications is required. It is quite possible to work with the analysis without taking on board the underlying assumptions. Where the different advocates are developing pedagogical techniques these must be impacted by the deeply held views on the nature of learning possibilities.

Consider, for example, the VAK approach. Key protagonists include Gregorc, and Dunn and Dunn. They hold that learning styles are largely genetically determined and the individual preferred learning style, whether visual, auditory or kinesthetic, is therefore immutable. There are variations on this model that seek to extend it by combining the styles in pairs, but the assumptions remain largely the same. From this starting point it becomes imperative that the preferred learning style is established and a programme of teaching should be developed that supports the individual. For the visual learner an emphasis would be placed on maps, charts, images and DVDs, and utilize mind mapping. For the auditory learner there would be an emphasis on paired work, discussions, tapes, music and mnemonics. For the kinesthetic learner field trips would be useful, the learning would be very much experiential: learning through doing. This is a well-worn pathway that has been utilized by many teachers.

There has been a ready capitulation to the assumptions about the use of VAK. Is it simply the way things are, and the teacher's task is to discover the preferred learning style and allocate strategies accordingly? Imagine entering a school and being sorted on the basis of being left or right handed and being constrained on that basis. To recognize that someone is right handed or left handed does not mean that the other hand is redundant. Indeed many tasks require high levels of integrated activity, for example playing the guitar usually necessitates the left hand operating at a more sophisticated level than the right.

There is a case for exposing the individual to a variety of inputs to ensure that those learning styles that are 'subordinate' develop and do not atrophy. The enthusiasm with which VAK has been embraced runs this risk of, and could encourage students into, withdrawing from aspects of a lesson because it does not relate to their particular style. To step even a short way down this path would be a significant disservice to an embryonic lifelong learner who will not always be able to indicate their preference in a future employment context. Many people remembering the tragedy of 9/11 will have predominantly visual memories. For those not close to the event, the experience was mediated through video footage; there was little alternative.

One of the originators of Neuro-Linguistic Programming (NLP), Michael Grinder (1989), concludes that in a typical class of 30 students 22 will be fairly balanced in their ability to take in information in a variety of ways. They will generally be able to cope with its being presented in visual, auditory or kinesthetic formats.

He argues that two or three of the students will have difficulties because of factors outside the classroom. Of the remaining six students, some 20 to 30 per cent will be either 'visual only' or 'auditory only' or 'kinesthetic only' learners. It is this significant minority who will have considerable difficulty in absorbing information unless it is presented in their preferred style. Grinder describes these constrained learners as 'VOs' (visual only), 'AOs' (auditory only) and 'KOs' (kinesthetic only). He suggests that it is not just coincidence that the initials 'KO' also stand for 'knockout'. He argues that these students are 'knocked out' of the educational system. He concludes:

 In every study I have seen regarding 'kids at risk', kinaesthetics make up the vast majority of the drop out rate.

(Grinder, 1989: page 79)

If Grinder is correct then the majority of students will still work in a learning context that is not sympathetic to their preferred style of learning. Every teacher, however, comes across the individual who cannot grasp a particular issue. The spectre of standing in front of the teacher's desk and having a mathematical glitch sorted out using pencils is already starting to loom. In such situations the longer the process goes on the more tense the learner becomes. Increasing stress is not a fertile seedbed for learning. In such a situation the grasp of the individual's preferred learning style could well provide the cognitive leverage to resolve the block.

Certainly VAK emphasizes the range of information channels. Teaching can be so easily conceived, in a limited sense, in terms of the lesson. There are rich opportunities to develop the cognitive environment; primary specialists have been good at this whereas, often, at secondary levels the provision of a multisensory learning environment has been less secure. Posters tend to change when they are ripped or immediately in advance of an Ofsted inspection.

The philosophical implications of Gardner's multiple intelligence construct have been raised earlier in the chapter. Some members of the educational community have embraced multiple intelligences (MI) with unbridled enthusiasm. Some schools in America market themselves as MI schools. There is even one LEA in England that is exploring the possibility of combining specialist schools with a MI selection process at the end of Key Stage 2. This would mean that a student demonstrating high levels of intelligence in the musical area would transfer to one school and a student demonstrating bodily–kinesthetic intelligence would presumably go to a specialist sports college. Of course, Gardner never suggests that the highlighted intelligence was restricted to one; he has always argued for several being more heightened. This would leave the super-selective process in some level of strain, unless at least 49 combination specialist schools were available. The question should also be asked: what provision would be appropriate for those displaying interpersonal and intrapersonal intelligences?

There is the additional problem of the age at which such intelligences become clearly demonstrated. Interviews with individuals who have demonstrated exceptional specific abilities often testify to understanding their ability in the sphere of excellence later in life.

There is a need to develop all-round competence, developing each area of intelligence. There must be the opportunity to enhance all areas in order to equip the individual for lifelong learning and also to feel secure within a rapidly changing world and society. It is desirable and wholly appropriate to develop all areas of ability, but this does not justify a levelling mediocrity. Gardner's perspective should allow for the recognition of specific areas of enhanced cognition and support these with 'master classes'. In some ways this is encompassed by the 'gifted and talented' initiatives. These do, however, generate a slightly uneasy feeling. In some instances they are wedded to the view of generalized intelligence rather than the development of specific strengths. The question must be asked as to how the remainder relate to being 'badged', by implication, 'the ungifted and untalented'.

Learning styles, relationships and rapport

Dr Barbara McCoombs (University of Denver Research Institute), a senior research scientist in the area of human motivation, has conducted research into student achievement. The research was conducted in the USA and involved a sample of 30,000 students and examined the contributory factors that supported their achievement. It was conducted across a range of students corresponding to Key Stages 1 to 4.

Dr McCoombs' (1999) work identifies four key dimensions or, in her terminology, domains by which teachers contribute to enhanced student achievement. These are:

- adapt to individuals: in essence this corresponds to learning styles;
- encourage higher-order thinking;
- honour the student voice: space and recognition is given for students' own opinions with curriculum related outcomes and also within the wider context of the school;
- create positive relationships.

The outcome of her research is that the area of relationships is the most significant contributory factor in supporting student achievement. The results of her work are summarized in Figure 5.1.

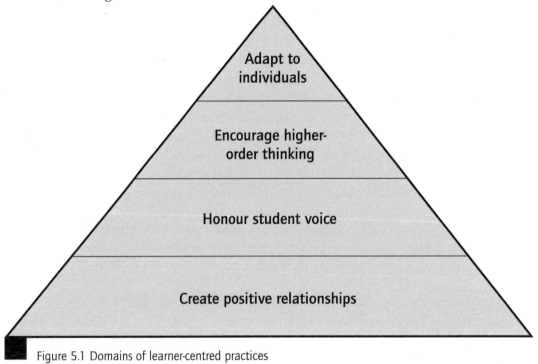

Figure 5.1 Domains of learner-centred practices

Perhaps surprisingly, the domain 'adapt to individuals' was understood as being less influential. In this model perhaps three out of four domains – adapt to individuals, honours student voice and create positive relationships – are not so far removed from each other.

Earlier the work of Michael Grinder was cited. Working with Richard Bandler he developed Neuro-Linguistic Programming (NLP). Their work centred on analysing human excellence and researching into how human beings go about making sense of their experience and interacting with others. Their initial work looked at the work of gestalt therapist Fritz Perls, therapist Virginia Satir and the psychotherapist Milton Erikson.

NLP is wide ranging in terms of its scope and techniques. One area that did emerge as extremely influential in terms of the ways in which people interrelate is the concept of 'rapport'. Rapport is the establishment of a responsive relationship and significantly functions at the subconscious level. It is argued that we like people who are like us or who are like the people we want to be. When people meet they normally search, usually through questions, to find connectivity. If you think of the behaviours exhibited at a party they are (well some at least) linked to finding connections between people through such areas as occupation, where we live, hobbies, children and even the journey to the party. Behaviours that are held to contribute to the establishment of rapport include:

- facial expression

- eye contact

- posture

- movements of the hands and legs

- keywords in speech

- breathing.

While these behaviours are frequently considered in the context of learning, it is likely that they make a significant impact in the establishment and maintenance of rapport. The NLP literature cites the learning or representational styles of auditory, visual and kinesthetic as central to establishing rapport. It would seem that when there is sensitivity towards the preferred learning style of another then rapport is supported. The use of language appropriate to the learning style, such as the language of hearing or seeing, or movement and feeling, will encourage rapport and help secure the engagement of learner and teacher.

Lack or loss of congruence breaks rapport very quickly and, as a consequence, will tend to result in the learner becoming detached or disengaged from the learning process.

This is a dimension of learning styles that is not generally explored in an educational context. While it is not suggested that it is the panacea for establishing constructive learning behaviours it deserves to be brought on to the agenda.

Taking learning styles further

At present there are substantial amounts of information about learning and about learning styles. Developing an understanding of learning and the understanding of learning styles is currently at a crossroads. At the time of writing, it is not a comfortable place to be. There is a great deal of ambiguity, claim and counter-claim. The movement to a more coherent understanding of learning styles is not supported by claims to have found the philosopher's stone and presenting a model not as a contribution to the debate but as the authoritative statement on the subject.

One of the most fruitful areas for coming to a greater understanding about learning is to ask the clients. While this will often not be expressed in technical language, it will not fail to be illuminating and developmental. Individual interviews, focus groups and simple feedback from a whole class about learning can provide considerable insight. It is important to structure this carefully. A technique used with leadership teams in industry and education is 'what went well?' (WWW) and 'even better if' (EBI). This simple technique analyses the situation and provides for improvement; it prevents a negative lancing of the 'cognitive boil'.

It has been argued that the issues around learning styles are complex and contentious. There are too many people peddling 'snake oil' and regrettably, perhaps because of the pressure to perform, too many willing to buy into simplistic answers. At the time of writing, learning and learning styles are part of the journey and not the destination. It would be valuable indeed if schools established conduits to allow the findings of research to be available to those engaged in developing and supporting the learning of children.

Case Study

Two Waters Primary School is a one-form entry primary school situated on the outskirts of Hemel Hempstead, Hertfordshire. It is a community focused school.

At Two Waters great emphasis is placed on teaching and learning and the importance of developing lifelong learners. The school constantly strives to establish a community of learners where a spirit of enquiry, reflection and risk-taking prevails. To support this they have abandoned worksheets and pupil textbooks and have empowered the children to generate their own work by creating their own questions and challenges.

This innovative approach to learning has lead to a range of strategies being used, which include working partners, thinking skills, accelerated learning and the use of preferred learning styles across the curriculum. A Year 6 boy said: 'I am a visual learner. Being visual helps me a lot because I can use lovely colours to make things easier to see and find.' Another child stated: 'In Year 6 we have songs to do with different areas of maths which really helps because they pop into your head when you need them.' Another visual learner said: 'I use colour a lot in English because when it comes to a test I can remember what I did in that lesson.'

Children and staff are aware of their preferred learning styles and also of the need to develop their weaker styles in order to broaden their approach to learning. As well as the use of visual, auditory and kinesthetic styles, multiple intelligences are incorporated so that our lessons are multisensory and engage the children's curiosity.

The idea of triple coding has recently been introduced in order to provide the children with an anchor for their learning. This is based on Marilee Sprenger's work on 'differentiation through learning styles and memory'. Within the lesson there are opportunities to use visual, auditory and kinesthetic sensory pathways. Each child chooses an activity, which will be linked to his or her preferred learning style. At the end of each session the children are asked to think of an anchor, which will enable them to recall the information used. For example, it might be that they will remember the smell of the teacher's perfume, or the school dinner smell wafting across the school! It may be where the teacher was standing in the room or what he or she was wearing, or it could be using their sense of touch if it was a D&T (design and technology) session. It is hoped that this will help children's long-term memory and enable them to recall facts when they are faced with a test situation throughout all of their education.

Nanette Paine, Headteacher

Chapter 6

Assessing personalized learning

Max Coates

Introduction

Any discussion of assessment is like crossing a minefield. It is a concept riddled with deeply held assumptions about its purpose and use; it is an area of competing and conflicting intentions and often relates to views about the nature of education that are divergent. In England and, indeed, in many other countries it has strong links with a centralized and target-driven educational system. The dominance and consequences of assessment processes also have a high impact on workload and morale.

There remains a significant emphasis on summative assessment. In essence, this is the measurement of the output of the educational process typified by SATs (scholastic assessment tests) regimes at ages seven, 11, 14 and by GCSE and AS and A2 examinations. These serve as 'gatekeeper' qualifications for students and, of course, are used to hold teachers, schools and local education authorities to account.

The impact of testing on teaching and learning

The higher the stakes that flow from the testing the greater will be the likelihood that teachers will feel impelled to teach to the test. Paul Black (1998) cites this quote from the last century:

> *Not a thought was given, except in a small minority of schools, to the real training of the child, to the fostering of his mental (and other) growth. To get him through the yearly examination by hook or by crook was the one concern of the teacher. As profound distrust was the basis of the policy of the Department, so profound distrust of the child was the basis of the policy of the teachers. To leave the child to find anything out for himself, to think anything out for himself, would have been regarded as incapacity, not to say insanity, on the part of the teacher, and would have lead to results which, from the percentage point of view, would probably have been disastrous.* (Holmes, 1911 (cited in Black, page 12))

This quotation, from nearly 100 years ago, engenders intense feelings of déjà vu. It is beyond the scope of this chapter to tunnel too deeply into the dislocated world of assessment. The focus is unashamedly on the essential contribution that assessment, particularly formative assessment, can make to the growth of confident and cognitively proficient learners: learners who understand mistakes as stepping stones and not walls, and learners for whom constructive feedback is germane to their progression to becoming autonomous learners. Assessment for personalizing learning acknowledges that it should occur as an integral part of teaching and learning and that the information gained from assessment activities can be used to further shape the teaching and learning process.

Facing some of our beliefs about assessment

A cursory examination of the history of testing soon reveals that one of the main drivers has been a desire by society to grade its workforce. In 1916, Lewis Terman, at Stanford University, developed the Stanford–Binet IQ test, which became the antecedent to subsequent IQ tests. Terman and others argued for the use of this test with the general populace and not just for its use with the minority that have learning difficulties. The chance to use it in a wholesale fashion came with America's entry into the First World War. A version of the IQ test was combined with multiple-choice techniques and used to test 1.75 million soldiers – there was a need to assess large numbers who were recruited with no accompanying details of existing proficiencies.

Underpinning the use of these tests were the beliefs that, because they were scored and externally marked, they were inherently objective. It was believed that they were capable of measuring the individual's intelligence and potential. They were, in fact, actually measuring the individual's equivalent of a computer's central processing unit (CPU).

Testing regimes, like IQ tests and other close relatives, draw on particular models of learning that are rooted in the early part of the twentieth century. It is argued that two assumptions underlie these, which are founded on the idea of instruction: decomposability and decontextualization (Gipps, 1994).

The first of these concludes that complex competencies could be broken down into constituent skills, each being learned separately through stimulus – response learning. Indeed, some simple tasks can be learned in this way, for example elementary mathematical calculations. Most complex skills do not, however, function this way. They are not sequential but rather are interconnected. This complexity holds true from activities as varied as reading a novel to riding a bike.

The second assumption of instructional theory is decontextualization. This holds that each of the constituent components of a complex skill remains fixed regardless of where it is used. Current understanding indicates that there is a very close connection between the skill and the setting or context in which it is used.

> *Educationally this suggests that we cannot teach a skill component in one setting and expect it to be applied automatically in another. That means, in turn, that we cannot validly assess a competence in a context very different from the context in which it practiced or used.* (Resnick and Resnick, 1992: page 43)

This mode of thinking about learning as a mastery of collections of bits of information, and the collusion that multiple-choice type testing has contributed, has promoted shallow learning. Evidence has also shown that it does not support retention either. David Perkins (1992) of Harvard University asked several thousand people to take notes for discussions on general topics, such as the outcomes of violence on TV. These notes were then scored in terms of the standard of the arguments used. Astonishingly, he found little difference between high school dropouts and those with more advanced levels of education right through to postgraduates. He concluded that most educational practice does little to prepare students for reasoning about open-ended issues.

Current learning theory suggests that the instructional approach, which holds that knowledge is transmitted unchanged from teacher to student, is inadequate. Disparate facts detached from a conceptual framework quickly evaporate from the memory because they have neither meaning nor cognitive location.

> *Meaning makes learning easier, because the learner knows where to put things in her mental framework, and meaning makes knowledge useful because purposes and applications are already part of the understanding.* (Shepard, 1992: page 319)

This perspective of learning, where information is built into webs or networks that are not discrete but branch and chain in many directions, is derived from cognitive and constructivist psychology. Constructivism views learning as a process in which the learner actively constructs or builds new ideas or concepts based upon current and past knowledge. Constructivist learning, therefore, is a very personal endeavour, whereby internalized concepts, rules and general principles may consequently be applied in a practical real-world context. According to Jerome Bruner and other constructivists, the teacher acts as a facilitator who encourages students to discover principles for themselves and to construct knowledge by working to solve realistic problems, usually in collaboration with others. Cognitive theorists, such as Jean Piaget, David Ausubel and others, are concerned with the changes in a student's understanding that results from learning and with the fundamental importance of the environment. Constructivism itself has many variations, such as generative learning, cognitive apprenticeship, problem-based (enquiry) learning, discovery learning and situated learning. Regardless of the variety, constructivism promotes a student's free exploration within a given framework or structure.

If learning is merely a transmission of information, then testing is about checking if the installation is correct: have the appropriate facts been remembered? A key learning strategy must be memorization, and a key assessment strategy could well be the multiple-choice test. On the other hand, constructivist approaches are evident within classrooms to varying degrees. They are inherently linked to the development of deep learning, which is characterized by:

- an intention to understand material for oneself;

- interacting vigorously and critically with the content;

- relating ideas to previous knowledge and experience;

- using organizational principles to integrate ideas;

- relating evidence to conclusions;

- examining the logic of the argument (Entwistle, 1992).

If this pathway is followed and deep learning is held to be desirable then development of such learning will require reflection on the processes by which new knowledge is being created. This process is termed metacognition. In this view of learning, process becomes the leading partner to content. The change, in turn, will require new assessment methodologies.

Tests ought not to ask for demonstration of small, discrete skills practiced in isolation. They should be more ambitious instruments aimed at detecting what mental representations students hold of important ideas and what facility students have in bringing these understandings to bear in solving their problems.
(Shepard, 1991: page 9)

No gold watches

One of the casualties in our changing world must be the manufacturers of gold watches. It must be very rare that the inscribed gold watch is given as a long-service award. Rather our world is a global one, dominated by advances in technology and communications change is its hallmark. Gipps (1994) suggests that:

In many industrialized countries the call is the same, for workers at all levels who can operate and understand technical systems, and be flexible, adaptive learners since we are educating a generation of pupils who rather than have a trade or career for life as in our parents' and grandparents' day, are likely to have one or more changes of task and conditions of work during their working lives. The call is for schools to provide programmes that enable students to reason and think, not just perform routine operations. This move, to require thinking and problem solving programmes for all students rather than just for the elite or high achieving students, is new: the higher order skills of interpreting unfamiliar texts, constructing convincing arguments, developing approaches to problems etc. have been in the British and American systems, reserved for the elite. (pages 25–26)

The question that must at some point be asked is: is it more important to remember information or to remember where it can be accessed and used to create meaning? Revision is not about competence and is arguably not a valued skill in the world of work.

Assessment for learning and life

The argument has been made that learning is a complex process, which is personally constructed and non-linear. Further, that the process is at least, if not more, important than content. Finally, that the skills for employment are related more to the activity of thinking than to the activity of remembering.

Consider a visit to the doctors. A range of objective measurements are used, for example blood pressure, pulse rate, haemoglobin count and many more. Usually a diagnosis is reached through an interaction of these test procedures with the professional judgement of the doctor. A similar model seems less acceptable in the world of education; the teacher is not given the same extensive remit to assess the condition of the patient. There are several reasons for this:

- In part this has evolved from the beliefs that are held about the nature of intelligence and ability that have come from instructional models and the myth of the validity and objectivity of external testing.

- The perception that teachers as a profession do not have a grasp of the nature of learning and so cannot be considered sufficiently skilled to make appropriate judgements.

- The linking of education to political rhetoric and economic performance fuels a drive for allegedly 'hard data' about student and institutional performance.

To change the landscape there must be a committed journey by teachers to develop a community of practice around the understanding of learning. Schools should encourage the development of action learning sets that take an understanding of learning beyond the mythology and engage with the changing horizons of cognition. From this understanding then develop activities that support learning and provide a platform for supporting formative assessment. There is a need to develop the culture of formative assessment to support the student's journey and reduce the emphasis on the harder edged summative assessment that could well reveal, too late, that they have arrived at the wrong destination.

While appropriate and carefully constructed tools are essential in developing formative assessment, studies also place great emphasis on the nature of the feedback. Black and Wiliam (1998) presented formative assessment as:

> ... all those activities undertaken by teachers, and/or their students, which provide information to be used as feedback to modify teaching and learning activities in which they are engaged. (page 7)

It has often been noted that not all feedback has significant impact in terms of taking learning forward. Sadler (1989) concludes that for feedback to be effective there must be a clear understanding of the intended goal or standard coupled with an understanding of how current performance relates to this and an awareness of the necessary strategies which will close the gap between the two. Consider the following taken from a recent Year 11 report:

> Stephen has continued to work well. In the exam, he must ensure that he writes to the task and checks the accuracy with which he expresses his ideas. Orally his progress has been excellent. Stephen's thoughtful and sustained personal interpretations of the text helped him to get a good grade in the English literature exam. He needs to consider the requirements of the task more carefully. His excellent efforts and abilities deserve matching results in the summer. (January 2005)

The mock examination result was cited as 'B' and with effort an 'A*' could be achieved at GCSE. The strategy for transformation is not immediately clear. This is the same student, mentioned elsewhere, who has not actually read the texts but has worked from synopses downloaded from the internet. A great deal of time and effort goes into producing school reports, but in what way are they a potent force for change?

Ofsted says some reports are bland and useless

> Inspectors have urged teachers to heed their own advice about good writing and stop filling pupils' reports with 'bland' remarks such as 'could do better'.

> The Office for Standards in Education said secondary teachers needed to give parents more detail about children's strengths and weaknesses and say how they measured up against national standards.

Ofsted warned that pupil assessment was good in only a third of secondary schools, and that poor report-writing and a lack of constructive marking were to blame. David Taylor, Ofsted director of inspection, said: 'It's not just good enough to say "He has had a good term doing satisfactory work." We should be talking about targets and a sense of the individual things that pupils can work on to really improve.'

The Ofsted study on assessment showcases 12 schools that assess well. Examples of comments that are seen as being good practice include: 'She could improve her anticipated grade to A* if she practises sketching graphs from equations' and 'He must extend his background knowledge by using secondary sources of information to expand his notes'.

The Qualifications and Curriculum Authority has launched an advice page on report-writing on its website, and is inviting teachers to give feedback. It urges teachers to write in a clear and straight-forward way and to ensure that reports are personalized. (TES, 2003)

The extract above, taken from the *Times Educational Supplement* (TES), assumes that it is the neglect of feedback that is the problem. There is the almost tacit assumption that quality and impact may be taken for granted; if only that were the case. My own work with senior and middle leaders suggests that we are a long way from establishing a culture of constructive feedback in our schools. Torrance (1993) has expressed concern that the use of formative assessment for feedback is often expressed in terms of unrealistic generalizations phrased in less than concrete terms.

The process of giving feedback is problematical; it utilizes a complex skill-set similar to that associated with mentor coaching. At the heart of the process lie empathy, active listening and the ability to ask questions rather than give answers. The professionally informed-telling mode is unlikely to promote deep learning, though it has its place in supporting legitimate shallow learning. A question might not be the appropriate response to 'Where are the safety goggles?' in a science lesson. Equally, a statement might not be the most enabling comment when asked: 'How could I make the conclusion about the effect of light on the rate of photosynthesis in pondweed a better one?' Dialogue and reflection are powerful tools.

Another article from the *Times Educational Supplement* links to Black and Wiliam's (1998) work supporting the view that sometimes the apparently obvious is not actually the case:

Forget about the marks, focus on feedback

Pupils' national test and GCSE results improved by more than half a grade when teachers stopped giving marks out of ten and gave children detailed feedback, research shows.

The study is a boost for the 'assessment for learning' technique which is gaining support.

David Hargreaves, former head of the Qualifications and Curriculum Authority and adviser to education secretary Estelle Morris, is also a fan.

The study was led by professors Dylan Wiliam and Paul Black of King's College London. They say tests and targets do not in themselves raise standards and that quality feedback from teachers is crucial.

Six schools in Medway and Oxfordshire tried the techniques in maths and science classes. Parallel classes, often taught by the same teacher, were monitored. When GCSE results and national test scores were compared, the assessed classes gained the equivalent of just under half a level at Key Stage 3 and more than half a grade at GCSE.

The findings support an earlier review of 600 pieces of research from around the world, involving 10,000 pupils.

Usually, when given grades or marks for homework, pupils look only at these and ignore suggestions for improvement. So the teachers concentrated on giving only comments, on which pupils were expected to take action to improve the work. This shifted attention away from competing for marks and merits, and towards each using the opportunity to produce their best work. Two of the schools now have a school-wide policy that no marks or grades are given on homework. (TES, 2002)

I would suggest that there is also confusion in the minds of many teachers about the nature and impact of praise when giving feedback. We have come to be fascinated with self-esteem and its potential link with achievement. The assumption is that if we raise self-esteem, achievement will follow in its wake. The reality is much more complex, rather like the link between wealth and happiness; not having wealth may make you unhappy but equally having it may not guarantee happiness.

Positive esteem does not guarantee high motivation, neither is it essential for self-motivation.

Self-esteem is often thought of as something teachers can nurture in students by, for example, praising their good features and protecting them from their deficiencies. But this may just be pretending their difficulties do not exist and will not help them cope with setbacks. Focusing on self-esteem may only offer the student ways to avoid facing up to and learning from their problems and mistakes.

Damage to self-esteem has adverse effects on everyone and we all want to avoid this. Trying to raise students' self-esteem directly, however, may have limited success as this ignores the fact that many of our feelings about ourselves come from what we do rather than cause us to do it. (McLean, 2003: page 48)

Schools do not directly influence self-esteem as much as they often believe. The largest single source of variation in self-esteem is genetic, which may contribute one-third of the whole (Kendler et al., 1998). Perhaps the major impact of feedback in this area is the potential to damage fragile self-esteem with negative, sarcastic or even thoughtless comment.

Feedback related to formative assessment needs to avoid gratuitous praise, which can encourage the demonstration of ability rather than developing learning. The development of belief in change and progress through time will support confident learning, whereas inculcating belief that ability is allocated is unlikely to support autonomous confident learners. Carefully constructed, constructive and challenging feedback can communicate high expectations, while superficial praise for easy success can convey disinterest.

David Cooperrider cites the heliotropic hypothesis, which states that

> *Human systems have an observable tendency to evolve in the direction of those positive images that are brightest and boldest, most illuminating and promising.*
> (Cooperrider et al., 2003: page 12)

He also contrasts this with the nature of our inner dialogue. He suggests that all humans exhibit an ongoing internal film show or inner dialogue. In essence, we play a film show of future possibilities. Where this has an equal ratio of images of future possibilities, of positive to negative, we move towards being dysfunctional, where the ratio exceeds two positive to each negative there is functional confidence. Feedback provides information about progress, but it also supports the development of images of the future, which develop intrinsic motivation.

Peer assessment

Black (1998) suggests that there are practical as well as fundamental reasons why it is legitimate that students have a role in assessment. At the practical level he argues that this would free teachers to engage in more formative assessment and consequently more feedback to their students. The more fundamental argument is that by assessing their own and indeed the work of others it will compel the student to understand more comprehensively and support the development of their own metacognition.

It is also clear that an ad hoc arrangement will not serve to advance learning; it is unlikely that competence will be gained immediately. Black gives one example of the development of student-led assessment in science. It was noted that it took a year for students to use it productively and move from vague comments to ones that were more meaningful. Black concludes that this was because they were not used to thinking about their own learning and also because they had to change their mindset away from the concept of the formal teacher-led test.

Case Study

Peer assessment

Teacher E approached formative assessment by first dividing up the Y10 topic of human nutrition, circulation and excretion into three blocks of work. He knew that his class already had quite a sound grounding in nutrition and circulation because of the work that they had done in Y9 and before. Excretion was less well known and he decided to use the teaching of this topic as a way of linking together all three areas to help his class transfer knowledge from one area to another. So he decided to cover nutrition and circulation quickly, mainly through a circus of quick practicals, demonstrations and videos. Homework tended to be questions given on worksheets, which checked that the pupils were getting detailed notes on each part of the work.

After four one-hour lessons and two homeworks, pupils were asked to revise the work done so far for the next lesson. They were told that it was not for a test but for something that required better understanding than a test.

Next lesson, the class were split into groups of five. Each group was given a set of five cards, each of which had one of the following words at the top: Absorption, Blood, Circulation, Digestion, Enzymes. The cards were randomly distributed in the groups and the pupils were told that they would have just over five minutes to produce a short oral presentation on that aspect of the topic which they would then give to the other four members of their group. To help them focus their presentations, underneath each heading were around four pointers as to what to include. For example, the Blood card said:

- What are the main components of blood?

- Briefly, what job does the plasma do?

- Briefly, what job do the red blood cells do?

- How do white blood cells defend the body against pathogens?

After the preparation time, the teacher stopped the children and told them how they were going to judge each other's presentations in their group. They secretly had to 'traffic light' each presentation and give details to justify their decision as follows:

> **Green** = better than I could have done it/I learned something from this.
>
> **Amber** = about the same as I could have done it/no major omissions or mistakes.
>
> **Red** = not as good as I could have done it/some omissions or mistakes.

The order for presentations was alphabetical. Feedback was not given within the group until all five presentations had been done. So each member of the group judged four presentations and was given four feedbacks from his or her peers on his or her presentation. The pointers on the cards became rough criteria that supported the discussion and sometimes disagreement about the traffic light colour given. Through the dialogue pupils were able to decide on more sophisticated criteria for their judgements. For example, one pupil who had an Enzyme card had responded to the card detail of saying what they are by saying that they were 'biological catalysts'. The others in the group decided that he should also have said that enzymes were also proteins because that helped later when explaining why enzymes do not function at high temperatures.

The teacher then facilitated a five-minute whole-class discussion where some pupils were selected to explain why their presentation had not been awarded 'green' and what they needed to do to improve. Pupils who accepted that they were 'red' or 'amber' for their presentations were then asked to write out an improved version of their presentation in their books. Those pupils who were 'green' were asked to select the card that they felt least confident about from the remaining four and do a written presentation on that topic. The teacher circulated as the written work was being completed, stopping at each table and checking with some individuals that they were clear what they needed to include. Those who finished before the end of the lesson were asked to read one another's work to check that they had included all the points.

Assessment is for Learning, 2005 – Project 1

Accrediting assessment

To a significant extent, the need to accredit assessment is linked to summative assessment. There are various requirements to know how 'good' a particular student is with reference to a given subject, skill or competency. Questions are often asked as to how secure such judgements might be when set against geographical origins or across time. Comparisons are being made in many areas, for example doctors from some countries are allowed to practise in the UK without supplementary study and examinations while other have to undergo what amounts to retraining. Consider public perceptions of the worth of A levels or degrees from the 1960s with those currently on offer. Accountability also affects the demand for objective summative testing. Politicians project themselves as champions of educational reform and require a measure of the impact of their policies. High-stakes testing, which is normally summative in nature, is used as a coercive lever to change the climate of performance.

For many, movement away from the mythology of objectivity is unimaginable. When the teacher-driven Certificate of Secondary Education (CSE) was introduced in the 1960s it had a knock-on effect within the parallel General Certificate of Education (GCE) system. At least one examining board developed an experimental system, which allowed pupils to gain a GCE on the basis of coursework and teacher assessment. This innovative step did not survive long before its perceived threat to the assessment gene pool lead to a return to the safety of the examination. It is worth noting that this belief in the objective reliability of national or sub-national testing is by no means universal. In Australia, Queensland abandoned state-wide testing in 1982. In Sweden external final examinations were abandoned in 1971. New Zealand utilizes a combination of teacher assessment allied to a 'light sampling' approach, which allows for accountability and cross-school moderation.

Formative assessment, in its unadulterated form, stands outside the accreditation loop. The focus is about supporting learners and their development. In this role, it cannot fail to engage in the support of personalizing learning. To be effective, three components must coincide in formative assessment:

- There must be a consensus about the objective of the learning activity. This may well include content and skills, and should include a clear focus on the elements of metacognition. Simply put, if we are uncertain about our destination we cannot pass comment on the route.

- Appropriate strategies must be developed to support the formative assessment. These should be embedded in the learning process in its design phase. Formative assessment is not about expressing an opinion, it is about engaging in a rigorous professional activity, which drives learning. The case study outlined above shows one teacher's approach to this demanding dimension of education.

- Feedback to students must be effective. Giving transformative feedback is challenging and a competence that needs to be developed over time. It is unlikely to be an inherent personality trait in the assessor. Superficial feedback will not only be ineffective but could well prove detrimental, if McLean (2003) is to be believed.

While an individual teacher may demonstrate effective formative assessment, it is likely that it would flourish in a community of practice. A professional development day centred on formative assessment would also support deep learning on cognition and pedagogy. Formative assessment, with its unambiguous link to learning, is exciting because it draws close to the personalizing learning agenda. It is also likely to be inherently subversive because it fosters an understanding of assessment outside the scrutiny and constraints of national testing regimes.

Testing and motivation

The impact of assessment of testing on motivating students to learn has been touched on earlier in the chapter. It seems, however, useful to provide a summary of the work undertaken by Harlen and Deakin Crick (2002). In essence, this is a review of published research focused on summative assessment using the evidence for policy and practice information (EPPI) methodology. A widespread search found 183 studies which were potentially relevant. The focus was then narrowed down to 19, which were identified as providing sound and valid empirical evidence.

The review concludes that there is strong evidence that summative assessment has a negative impact on pupils' motivation for learning. The reviewers comment that:

> Many aspects of the impact have significant consequences for pupils' future learning, and thus have causes for concern. (page 2)

Three of the areas emerge strongly. First, the particularly detrimental impact that testing regimes have on pupils of low ability by confirming their own negative beliefs about learning. Second, that summative testing was causing teachers to teach to the test and inhibiting the development of higher-order skills. Third, the tests were favouring students who are linear sequential thinkers. The review underscores the impact of testing on learning and teaching. At the level of national policy, it must also call into question how such models of testing relate to the emphasis on personalizing learning.

Conclusion

Assessment is an integral part of learning, and the style and application can either enhance or diminish the learning that is taking place. Superficial assessment, which has its origins in psychometrics, will tend to lead to teaching to the test and shallow learning by pupils. Not only is such learning shallow, it tends not to achieve cognitive connection and produces knowledge without meaning, which is not readily transferred to other areas of experience.

The current educational dispensation in England has placed great store by summative testing. Extremely large sums of money have gone into the development of national testing schemes and their subsequent administration. PricewaterhouseCoopers was commissioned to complete a financial model of the English examination system. The report estimated that the cost of running the examination system in 2003–2004 was £610 million. This includes the £370 million cost of running the organizations involved in the exam system and £240 million of staff time in delivering the exam activities that are included in the scope of the model (Qualifications and Curriculum Authority, 2004a). MacLeod (1982) has observed that examinations are:

 … possibly the single most intrusive and expensive innovation in Western education in the last century. (page 16)

Is there an argument for changing the balance of spending and promoting assessment models, which actually facilitate learning?

> *We need to persuade politicians and policy makers of the importance of lowering the stakes associated with assessment whenever possible, particularly at the level of the teacher and the school. With assessment for certification and selection purposes, high stakes are unlikely to be reduced and therefore the style and content of assessment tasks is particularly crucial. We also need to persuade policy makers of their responsibility for evaluation of the educational and social consequences of test use at every level.* (Gipps, 1994: page 175)

Formative assessment links directly to personalizing learning. It has the capacity to stimulate deep learning. It will also enhance the skills of teachers and has the potential to set alight communities of practice and turn classrooms into learning laboratories.

Chapter 7

ICT and personalization

Max Coates

My youngest son, Stephen, is a pleasant, if slightly quirky, 15-year-old 'card-carrying' guitarist. I walked into his room recently and was fascinated by what I saw and heard. He was composing and playing a piece of music, which was then downloaded to one of his friends three miles away. The friend, a bass guitarist, added a further track and returned the recording. It was then transferred to the bedroom next door via a radio network, edited and recorded using an IT package.

Intrigued by what was going on, I tracked his use of ICT over the course of a week. The range of activity was astounding and included:

- Social discussion with friends and with a cousin in Canada using MSN (Microsoft Network).

- Buying and selling guitar components on eBay.

- Discussions in a specialist chatroom with other guitarists on the relative merits of different tremolo arms.

- Downloading construction details for a guitar project, including a routing template.

- Listening to the sound and performance of different pickups.

- Downloading music, both audio and tablature.

- Multi-tracking a composition for GCSE coursework.

- Researching history coursework.

- Obtaining synopses of English literature set texts (also obtaining a mock exam 'A' grade without actually reading the books, which seems somewhat subversive).

- Pastoral support of friends using MSN.

- Producing a PowerPoint presentation for a talk at a church youth event.

- Interchange of ideas on homework, even interchange of homework.

- Use of word-processing, spreadsheet and graphic packages for the completion of coursework.

- Revision using specialist websites.

- Editing a DVD for use in a national leadership programme (this paid for the guitar components).

- Booking cinema tickets online.

- Access to dictionary, thesaurus and concordance.

- Planning a musical set to be performed with friends later in the week.

This prompted discussions with a group of Stephen's teenage friends. There was a variation in activity but, in all cases, the scope was extensive. One of the group had recently been given his own show on a local radio station. He regularly uses ICT to generate and send 'jingles', which are used by the station on a variety of their programmes. Perhaps the most challenging image was that of this student taking a business call from the radio station on his mobile and holding the conversation under the desk during a GCSE English lesson. It takes the concept of links with industry to a whole new dimension.

In 1943, Thomas Watson, a director of IBM, concluded that 'There is room for about five computers on the global market', while *Popular Mechanics* magazine in 1949 prophesized that 'In the future computers will weigh just below 1.5 tons'.

These statements look ludicrous from our contemporary vantage point. It is certainly not the world in which these teenagers move and flow. It must be admitted that they all come from affluent homes, where ICT is freely available and broadband is commonplace. It is, however, likely that the IBM prediction has been exceeded in many of their individual homes. For them ICT is merely a tool. They have ceased to marvel at it and hold it in any sense of awe. The 'sting in the tail' is that the teenagers interviewed paid no debt of gratitude to the input in this area of their school. Their general conclusion was that, apart from network management, their grasp and usage was more creative and sophisticated than that presented in the context of their formal education. Further, the technology they had access to at school was frustrating and outdated. At the time of writing there are still schools using the original Acorn computers.

Much of the discussion about ICT has centred on processing power. We have moved through from the 286 to the Pentium with a similar mindset to that of moving from a Ford Fiesta to a Ferrari. This trend could well continue with the development of new generations of computers, including biochemical computers, which will allow more sophisticated software to run still faster. In practice, outright processing power is unlikely to be the primary focus of development. There will, however, be continuing issues relating to the ability of networks at local and global levels to carry the ever-increasing volume of traffic.

Ackling and Lowes (2004) produced a report for British Telecom entitled *Thriving in the Digital Networked Economy*. This highlights the pre-eminent role of connectivity. The picture of the future is of a 24/7 connected world that operates at a global level and does not recognize geographical boundaries. Globalization is not a prediction, it is a current reality and ICT provides the neurological system. In 2003–2004, in India, software and business process outsourcing (BPO) exports, the mainstay of industry, grossed US$12.5 billion, up from US$9.6 billion in 2002–2003, indicating a growth of 30.5 per cent for the year (Development Gateway, 2005). IT has already passed beyond the outsourcing of manufacturing and running of directory enquiries from a call centre in India. At the centre of these developments is connectivity at both the commercial and personal levels, which is not equitable; while the landscape is changing to the advantage of new players, such as India and China, many countries remain excluded. UN (United Nations) Administrator for Development, Mark

Malloch Brown (2000) spoke of 'information affluence' and the disparities that exist. He contends that:

> *The facts speak for themselves. Even more than income, goods or services, information is today predominantly the property of the rich world – and a thin slice of the rich world at that. Half the world has never used a telephone. Over 40% of the US now uses the internet – but just 1.6% of Asians and 0.3% of Africans do so. And when it comes to content, over 80% of web pages and 90% of documents on the web are in English despite the fact that the vast majority of the world does not speak it.* (Brown, 2000: page 1)

The BT report draws on Schumpeter to show how our society has gone through a series of transitions leading from 1785 when manufacturing was centred on iron, textiles and waterpower to the turn of the millennium and the emergence of an economy founded on digital networks and the flow of information. It argues that the power of the network increases exponentially with the number of computers connected to it. Further, each computer added to the network both uses it as a resource while at the same time adding resources, in a spiral of increasing value and choice. Additionally, there will be an increasing convergence of voice and data networks. It is likely that mobile phone masts will largely disappear as Bluetooth technologies 'daisy chain' our communications from phone to phone through the network.

The commercial world runs globally 24/7. Can formalized education remain engaged, utilizing a 7/5 model operating at a parochial level? The challenge becomes greater when we recognize that the client group, the students, frequently live locally and increasingly learn globally.

The current educational perspective on ICT

Much of the focus of the deployment of ICT seems to be at the structural level. The report by Ofsted (2004), *ICT in Schools: The Impact of Government Initiatives Five Years On*, offers eight main findings. These are summarized as follows:

- There has been an increase in the competence of staff in ICT with 90 per cent of teachers observed being competent in the use of ICT.

- The outcomes of the initiatives are more evidenced by pupil achievement in ICT than in other subjects.

- The gap between the best and the worst provision is unacceptably wide.

- The training provided by New Opportunities Fund (NOF) funding has been disappointing.

- Where schools provided ICT training this was generally more effective than NOF-funded training.

- The level of technical support for ICT varies widely between schools.

- There has been a significant increase in the connection of schools to broadband. However, it was noted that few schools had made significant use of applications specifically supported by broadband.

- There has been an improvement in the ICT support provided by local education authorities (LEAs).

A consideration of the Ofsted report or the report for the DfES *ICT in Schools Survey 2004* (Prior and Hall, 2004) shows that great emphasis is placed on the provision of hardware and the training of staff. In both reports impact is considered particularly from the point of view of usage. The DfES report, for example, majors in the area of the personal use of ICT made by senior leaders in their own teaching.

The current usage of ICT supports teaching rather than learning. Contemporary usage of ICT appears to concentrate on the following areas:

- Providing greater structure to the teaching process where ICT imposes a format on the content of a lesson. This can be an external package such as Curriculum Online or in-house materials based on a package such as PowerPoint where there is an inherent structure imposed by the software.

- Interactive resources that have their roots in the programmed learning that was tortuously explored in the 1960s and which has come of age through the power and flexibility of ICT. Programs such as SuccessMaker, which supports mathematics and literacy, have provided flexibility and pupil interactivity. The deployment of these integrated learning systems has often been ill considered by schools (Coates, 1999: pages 178–180).

- Access to information through the use of the internet to either eclectic or primary sites.

- Familiarization with industrial/commercial uses of ICT, such as Cubase in music or AutoCAD in technology.

- The support of the teaching of shortage subjects using ICT programs as, for example, the use of Maths Alive and interactive whiteboards delivered by non-specialist maths teachers at Key Stage 3.

- Assessment: this has been used for a number of years at many levels ranging from recording, analysis, target-setting and online testing,

In *Issues of ICT, School Reform and Learning-Centred School Design* the conclusion is reached that:

> The investment of ICT in education in the UK has been significant. There have been many successes, but little systemic impact has been made in genuinely transforming the teaching and learning environments of individual classrooms. The reasons for this are complex and manifold and reflect experiences around the globe in issues of school reform and improvement. (Gipson, 2003: page 26)

In the same report a similar concern is expressed:

> Around the globe, one of the strongest drivers for educational reform comes from the demand for schools to access and incorporate ICT as a means of transforming teaching and learning. Yet the missing link in many ICT planning decisions lies in a clear definition of what is going to be done with it beyond a broad notion that it is important and desirable. Often the implementation of ICT is externally mandated by government policy and education authority edict. As a result, the technology is frequently never fully utilized to support and enhance teaching and learning and thus improve learning outcomes. (Gipson, 2003: page 5)

There seems to be support for the view that these new technologies have been incorporated into existing practices of schooling. In the early days of their introduction, they were jealously guarded and used by the initiated few. I remember the introduction of the first computer into a comprehensive school in Gloucester in the late 1970s. Afternoon tea was served and a mysterious black box, about the size of a kitchen cupboard, was unveiled which had the processing power of a speaking birthday card.

The situation has clearly changed; access to computers is commonplace but it is still incorporated within the model of education that is dominated by the transmission of knowledge by the enlightened to the intellectually malnourished. At a recent training day on leadership, a secondary head in the south of England was concerned that learning had been included on a course. He vociferously stated that this was unnecessary: it was the job of primary schools to develop learning and that of the secondary to instil content. Arguably this was unwise in a cross-phase conference!

ICT and the development of thinking

Protagonists of the ICT revolution often make claims that technology supports the development of thinking itself. If a student does not have access to ICT in what way would they be disadvantaged and would their cognitive development be inhibited? Is the computer simply a tool operating at the dictate of its operator or does it shape cognition itself?

One starting point in considering this issue would be the work of Seymour Papert. It was in his lab at the Massachusetts Institute of Technology that LOGO, the logic-based programming language for children, was developed. Papert is a protagonist for its development and it has subsequently become enshrined in the UK National Curriculum. At the heart of Papert's work is a deeply felt resistance to computer-aided instruction and a strong advocacy for children using ICT for their own intellectual development.

In his early days Papert had worked with Jean Piaget researching the development of mathematical reason. Piaget has been seminal in the idea of constructivism, which has as its foundation the argument that children do not simply absorb knowledge but need to construct meaning for themselves in order to learn. Papert published his views in the influential book *Mindstorms* (1980). The following is taken from the essay which forms the introduction to the book and refers to the way in which, as a child, visualizing gear mechanisms had helped him understand mathematical functions:

> *My thesis could be summarized as: What the gears cannot do the computer might. The computer is the Proteus of machines. Its essence is its universality, its power to simulate. Because it can take on a thousand forms and can serve a thousand functions, it can appeal to a thousand tastes. This book is the result of my own attempts over the past decade to turn computers into instruments flexible enough so that many children can each create for themselves something like what the gears were for me.* (Papert, 1980: page ii)

Papert's influence has been far reaching in the development of educational software. Many of these packages support the assembling and re-arranging of information to allow learners to construct meaning for themselves. Papert described ICT programs operating in this way as 'mind tools'. Jonassen (2000) cites databases as an example of a mind tool where the structure and field content guides the student to think in an ordered, logical manner and in doing so develop and shape his or her own cognitive processes. For Jonassen these mind tools provide a scaffold for thinking that is beginning to sound more like Vygotsky than Piaget. There is a fine line between development and conformity. Certainly, there are many who are nervous of a knowledge regime structured according to a Bill Gates world view.

Wegerif (2003), who has written extensively in this area, considers the use of programming as a computer-based mind tool. He suggests the following, which are claimed as benefits from programming:

- Learning problem-solving, problem-finding and problem-management strategies, such as breaking a problem into parts or relating it to a previously solved problem, planning and the kind of diagnostic thinking involved in debugging.

- Practising formal reasoning and representation, such as considering all possible combinations and constructing mathematical models.

- Valuing positive cognitive styles (or habits of the mind), such as precision and reflectivity over impulsivity.

- Reinforcing enthusiasms and tolerances, such as persistence, and enthusiasm for meaningful academic engagement.

He suggests that while programming language has been widely used and evaluated in schools it has not supported significant changes in cognition. He claims that there is little if any evidence that the general skills gained can be transferred to other contexts without someone else, usually a teacher, facilitating the transfer of skills into other areas.

The construction of concepts using protocols such as Buzan's Mind Mapping® (1996) has been translated to an ICT format. While debate continues as to the efficacy of mind mapping, there is no evidence to suggest that it is more effective in a digital format. Although the challenge of learning ICT-based programs, such as MindMapper, may add another layer to the learning. There are parallels with a tool used in leadership courses called 'Brown Paper Planning'. This is a low tech, almost 'Blue Peter' style, approach to planning which is assembled from, surprisingly, rolls of brown paper, masking tape and Post-its. It is almost a parody of the sophisticated software project management tools, such as Microsoft Project 2003. It has a high impact on groups using it largely because it has a kinesthetic dimension. People stand and move. Mind mapping, with A3 paper and coloured pens, shares the same dynamic.

The evolution of 'homo zappiens'

An intriguing theory is advanced by Wim Veen from Delft University of Technology. He speculates about the e-generation as the generation:

- of the remote control and mouse

- of Riven, Atlantis, Planetarion, unreal tournament, SMS, chatrooms and PlayStation 1 and 2

- that talks gaming at breakfast and dinner, and has its mobile phones switched on the whole time

- for which learning is playing and having fun

- that can chat in three rooms at a time with different personalities

- that invents games without winners or losers, without a clear start or end, and creates its own rules and changes them whenever it likes

- that is skateboarding up the stairs, instead of down them

- that is surfing the waves of the sea, and snowboarding instead of skiing

- that considers school as a meeting place rather than a learning place (Veen, 2002).

Veen deploys the pun 'homo zappiens' to describe multi-tasking, electronically interfaced young people. He argues that 'homo zappiens' do not fit comfortably within the schools and are berated for having:

- short attention spans, 'they cannot even listen for five minutes'

- hyperactive behaviour, 'they cannot concentrate on one task at a time!'

- no discipline, crushing their calculators, forgetting their textbooks, not passing on letters from school to their parents

- no respect, 'they consider their teachers as their equals' (Veen, 2002).

'Homo zappiens' are able to multi-task: listening to music, texting, doing homework and surfing the net all at the same time. TV watching frequently involves changing from channel to channel. While this is intensely disturbing to the terminally mature, it would appear that the chunks of information, whether audio, visual or textual, are being constructed into meaningful knowledge.

Most traditional models of learning are linear (as shown in Figure 7.1). Knowledge is seen as having an established sequential pattern moving from one area to the next. This would be typified by a traditional textbook, where there is a movement from a beginning to a conclusion.

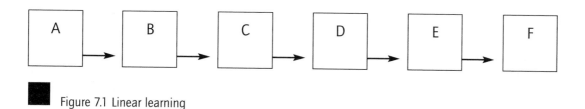

Figure 7.1 Linear learning

Veen argues that 'homo zappiens' are non-sequential learners moving potentially at random across subject disciplines, constructing unique mind maps from the information gained.

ICT can support non-linear learning. The web allows each person to construct his or her own journey through knowledge however conventional or idiosyncratic (as shown in Figure 7.2). What is less clear is whether ICT is creating this non-linear learning style or supporting an existing preferred approach to learning. Whatever the answer, there is a real sense that the 'genie is out of the bottle'. Teachers can no longer control the flow of information or its construction into an existing framework of meaning.

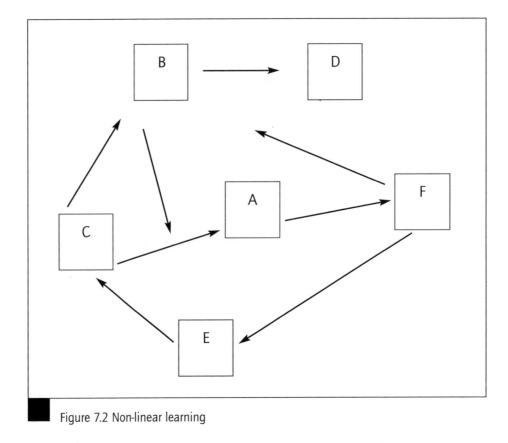

Figure 7.2 Non-linear learning

Veen also argues that there is considerable correspondence between these zappy, non-linear learners and the business world which also seems to function along similar lines. He argues that there is a 'strangle scenario' in the context of formal education that still tends to be very content driven and linear, and not connecting at a meaningful level with either the style and approach of their learners or the requirements of the business community.

The impact of computer games

Much of Veen's work appears plausible but is largely speculative. If the phenomenon of 'homo zappiens' is indeed alive and well and living in a town near you, he or she will undoubtedly be using ICT at some level to play games. Early review of student access to ICT was often optimistic because the students included dedicated games machines as computers.

Computer games may well impact the traditional curriculum-building expectations of the experience of learning which conventional everyday education cannot always meet. This is the conclusion of Kirriemuir and McFarlane:

> *Significantly the experience of game play seems to be affecting learners' expectations of learning activities. Preferred tasks are fast, active and exploratory, with information supplied in multiple forms in parallel. Traditional school-based learning may not meet these demands.* (2004: page 1)

Games come in different styles, from car racing, as in Gran Turismo, to role playing games, such as Final Fantasy. It has been argued that the former develop hand/eye co-ordination while the latter develop problem-solving, decision-making and strategy formulation. Wegerif (2003) has come to the conclusion that:

> *There is no evidence that games, or indeed any other software for that matter, can teach children thinking skills on their own. The important question to ask of students is not 'do they display thinking skills in what they are doing?' Of course they do. A better question is: 'what is the evidence that these skills will transfer in a useful way to other contexts in their lives?'* (page 12)

Perhaps the belief that gaming supports cognitive development is merely a comfort blanket for anxious parents.

Creativity and ICT

Defining creativity can be a challenge. One starting point might be *All Our Futures: Creativity, Culture and Education: The National Advisory Committee's Report* (DfEE, 1999). This report states that 'we are all, or can be, creative to a lesser or greater degree if we are given the opportunity'. The definition of creativity in the report is broken down into four characteristics:

> *First, they* [the characteristics of creativity] *always involve thinking or behaving* imaginatively. *Second, overall this imaginative activity is* purposeful: *that is, it is directed to achieving an objective. Third, these processes must generate something* original. *Fourth, the outcome must be of* value in relation to the objective. (page 29)

The Qualifications and Curriculum Agency produced a 'Creativity Pack', which concluded that pupils' creative thinking and behaviour could be identified as:

- questioning and challenging
- making connections and seeing relationships
- envisaging what it might be
- playing with ideas
- representing ideas
- evaluating the effects of ideas.

Much ICT advertising suggests that it will generate bright innovative possibilities and move us out of the grey conventional. Yet the undoubtedly creative Pablo Picasso was scathing about computers. He claimed, 'Computers are useless. They can only give you answers.' Perhaps some of the confusion over our use of computers comes from its frequent use as a metaphor for the human brain. There are some similarities between the computer and the brain. They both have inputs, process material and have an output, but then so does a university, a stomach and a toaster. Perhaps a better metaphor for the brain is that of a city with its multiple entry points, communities, wide range of activities and changing centres of operations. Meanwhile, the computer stands judged by standards it cannot attain, at least at present.

ICT can be used to develop material that is highly creative: consider for a moment the ICT-based input in the film version of Tolkein's trilogy *The Lord of the Rings*. At a more modest estimate, millions of people are using photographic, editing and graphic design packages supporting creative output. The operative word must remain support.

Loveless and Wegerif (2004) suggest that there are distinctive features of ICT that will support creativity. These are described as: 'provisionality', 'interactivity', 'capacity', 'range', 'speed', 'accuracy', 'quality', 'automation', 'multimodality', 'neutrality' and 'social credibility'. The provisionality enables changes to be made, alternatives tried and changes tracked. Interactivity engages users at a variety of levels, from the playing of games to monitoring changes over time. ICT has capacity and range allowing access to vast amounts of information across time zones and distance. Quality is supported in the potential of ICT to present and publish work to a high standard. Multimodality is the manner in which the user interacts text, image, sound and hypertextuality. Loveless and Wegerif are more cavalier in their description of neutrality and social credibility; with reference to the latter, that the superhighways are almost choked with biased and prejudiced material.

In the area of creativity, ICT is a tool that supports and allows change and enables experimentation without loss of the original; modelling becomes possible before execution. Tedium is the enemy of creativity and, where the process is interrupted by pedestrian tasks, creativity will be impeded. ICT, provided it does not become intrusive, can support flow.

ICT and motivation for learning

There is mounting evidence that supports teachers' intuitive feelings that ICT has a positive impact on student motivation (Becta, 2003). In research by Mosely and Higgins (1999) the use of ICT increases student motivation and engagement, and leads to learning gains in literacy and numeracy, The Notshool.net e-learning community was found to make a significant contribution to re-engaging 92 disaffected young people aged 14–19 (Duckworth, 2001).

Great care should be taken in reaching conclusions about why this is the case and in making assumptions that the deployment of ICT will inevitably resolve behavioural and motivational issues. Areas of impact made by ICT in the field of motivation for learning are suggested on page 93: emotional space; flexibility; and linkage to the future world.

Utilizing a more sophisticated pedagogy, there is enormous pressure on teachers to generate vibrant and effective lessons on a day-by-day basis. There is a serious potential for creativity overload. The deployment of ICT can introduce material that is visually and auditory engaging. However, as with any task, if it is too easy or too difficult, or even over used, motivation will decrease (Cox, 1997).

Students are engaging in learning using a technology in which they have ownership. They are frequently more confident in its use than the teachers. ICT is their territory and they walk through it with boldness, taking the operating intuitively and blazing their own trail.

They have the ability to draft and change: the phrase 'blotting one's copybook' is still in reasonably common usage. ICT allows for the production of a piece of work in a staged way, removing errors to move towards producing a finished piece of a higher standard. The significance of this dimension has been understated: ICT does not produce work with 'crossings out'.

Emotional space. Learning has a very strong social dimension but it also has intensity. Didactic confrontation remains a strong component within education, certainly in the UK. Engagement with ICT at an individual level can create personal space and in extreme cases even respite. Work in schools shows that ICT is often used as an activity for the student who has been withdrawn from lessons. This may underpin some of the reasons why its use has been constructive in responding to the impact of disaffected and disruptive students.

Flexibility. At its best, ICT supports the individual learning needs of students. Personal pathways become a possibility.

Linkage to the future world. ICT is self-evidently a requirement in the future world, the world beyond school. The link between many areas of curriculum content and the world of employment is not.

Motivation is a complex field but it is clear that ICT is making a positive contribution to student motivation and engagement. Improved motivation will inevitably lead to a student becoming an increasingly autonomous learner, having the confidence to develop his or her learning skills and accept the challenge of new learning.

The open garden

The picture presented so far has been of an almost limitless vista filled with unending and fascinating information ready to be welded into a new knowledge shape by a multitasking teenager. The true picture is less reassuring. The learner is about to join a field trip of learning that would not pass even a cursory risk assessment procedure.

Recently I discovered that a former resident of the area where I live had been a likely contender for the title of 'Jack the Ripper'. Having a passing interest in local history, I entered the information into a search engine. Incredibly, nearly 1.25 million potential sites were identified in 0.09 seconds. This led to some sites which were informative and even scholarly, but a large number was in the 'Elvis is still alive' category. (I admit I looked at that as well: 454,000 sites were suggested in a breathtaking 0.39 seconds.)

In order to integrate information to generate knowledge there must be confidence in the accuracy of the information and appropriate skills to evaluate its reliability and validity. Most people utilize search engines unless they know a specific site. The examples given above demonstrate the astonishing speed of these search engines. Some work by analysing keywords in any text; other search engines, such as Google, use a page rank (PR). This is a numerical ranking from 0 to 10, and is page specific, not site specific. The search engine calculates PR on a periodic basis for each and every page in its index. Google uses its proprietary (and secret) PageRank *Algorithm* to calculate your web page's PR based upon the *quantity* and *quality* of the links pointing to the page from other web pages. In essence, certain features will increase the chances of a given site being listed first. These factors will not necessarily be linked to reliability and validity. While search engines are extremely convenient they may well slant the range of information offered on a given topic. Website owners constantly try to determine the nature of the algorithm to increase their chances of selection, calling into question the objectivity of the information offered.

It is an understatement to say that the internet is a rich source of information, but the task of translating it is a challenge. For many students the temptation will be to access the sites offered first. The world wide web offers the opportunity to find information on any subject from all over the world. This accessibility can be both good and bad. Educators need to be aware of the reliability and validity of the information students are accessing. For example, a 14-year-old student wrote a history paper based on a website about how the Holocaust did not happen. He accepted the site at face value and used it as a single source for his essay. The Manhattan High Schools Superintendency (2002) produced a simple protocol to respond to the problem concluding that students need to consider three major things when assessing a web resource: authorship, publishing body and document information.

For others there will be a similar approach to the stamp collection in a biscuit tin: a large collection but no structure. Schools must develop strategies to improve the skills of concept building; while accepting statutory demands on curriculum structure there must also be the possibility of creating entirely new conceptual frameworks.

It is ironic that while this chapter was being written I had an extended conversation with a colleague on a problem of approaches to a teenager by a paedophile through a chatroom. The internet is both a private place, in that it is not easy for adults to monitor children, and a dangerous place. There is increasing evidence that paedophiles use the internet and that children, in their innocence, respond to them. Sixty per cent of online teens have received an email or internet message (IM) from a complete stranger and 63 per cent of those who have received such an email or IM say they have responded to strangers online. Overall, 50 per cent of those who use instant messaging, email or chatrooms have corresponded via IM or email with people that they have never met face to face (Weiss, 2003).

Fencing the garden is problematical and filtering technology can become intrusive: 'Nearly half the people survey (46%) say they have been blocked from non-pornographic sites by filtering technology' (Weiss, 2003). Education about the dangers may well prove more effective than electronics.

Conclusion

Computers have been in schools for over 20 years and still their contribution to learning remains unclear. Much of the discussion has centred on hardware and budget, with the learning impact being assumed. ICT can support many learning activities, such as handling data, research, presentation, drafting and creativity. It does not appear that it has the inherent ability to transform thinking. Indeed, it could actually constrain some learners by prescribing ways of doing tasks, creating the learner in its own image.

Commercially based institutions, beyond education, drive the technologies. Schools are consumers in a technology market that thrives on obsolescence. If we have moved so far in such a short time then can we forecast where we will be in a future similar period?

The commercial world works in teams where each individual contributes to the whole. Schools claim to focus on the individual but in fact educate them in cohorts and generic groupings. ICT is often used to corral the individual within a curriculum frame, while beyond school it is a world of fascinating connectivity without bounds constructed on impulse: a world that requires a mentor to support the generation of meaning and a guide to secure safe passage.

ICT has introduced an anarchic element into education where the students are more proficient in its use than many of those teaching. It subverts the learning order from knowledge transmission to personalized-knowledge creation. Regrettably, the students have not fully grasped the existing rules of the game and have become cognitively free range.

Case Study

Smart music

Aileen Monaghan, principal teacher of music at King's Park Secondary School in Glasgow, was a very worthy winner of a Becta ICT in Practice award. Here she reports on the success that she and her staff have achieved using ICT to help deliver the music curriculum.

When I first arrived at King's Park, I came from a background of ten years in music ICT consultancy work, and I was therefore keen to introduce ICT music facilities to a department that until then had none. With help from the headteacher and senior management, I obtained assistance from Glasgow City Council to turn the music department into a modern music technology facility.

Integrating ICT

The music department ICT development plan focuses on three main areas: the use of the internet, software tools and multimedia applications.

- The use of the internet allows pupils to source their own materials for listening projects, download appropriate MIDI (musical instrument digital interface) files and learn from the many exciting websites available.

- Software tools, such as Sibelius, Logic Audio and Cubase, allow pupils to produce a much more professional composition than was previously possible. Pupils also use Publisher and Word to improve the quality of their final folio presentations. This learning allows the music department to contribute to the generic skills that are needed in the workplace.

- Multimedia applications, such as GuitarCoach, provide pupils with extra help when their teacher is not available. These packages can be an extremely valuable aid to a busy classroom teacher.

Benefits for learners and staff

The new music ICT department at King's Park quickly showed positive improvements. Scottish Qualifications Association (SQA) results indicated an immediate improvement on those of previous years, and many more pupils wanted to take higher-still music courses. The behaviour of pupils improved, including the behaviour of the most challenging children in the school.

ICT allows staff to become more creative and confident. They can write appropriate individualized materials instead of buying books that often contain useful material in only certain chapters.

Staff are now part of lifelong learning strategies. Twenty years ago, many teachers left university feeling confident that they had all the skills needed to teach their subject. With the arrival of ICT new ways of learning are available. For the modern teacher this means two things: learning how to use the new ICT and then studying the best way of embedding it into the curriculum where appropriate.

Using ICT to raise educational standards

To achieve the process of embedding ICT at King's Park, we have rewritten the entire music syllabus.

- First- and second-year classes use many different CD-ROMs as part of their music course, and music sequencer packages are used by pupils to compose their own music. Busy lunchtime computer clubs are available twice a week to extend the time available to pupils.

- Higher and Standard Grade pupils write all music compositions on computers. Pupils can make CDs of their work, and all finished music is available for the examiner as a beautifully published score. Tutorials are available after school for more advanced study.

- The use of the smart board (interactive whiteboard) has allowed groups of 20 pupils to study computer-based music at a greater pace. CD-ROMs can be demonstrated to the whole class, with pupils controlling the clicks. The board has also been an excellent aid to improving the teaching of the electronic keyboard. The teacher can stand at the front of the class and press the appropriate note, allowing the pupils to see exactly what is being asked of them. For pupils with severe learning difficulties, sitting in one place for a long time is usually difficult. Getting them to take charge of the smart board is a great way to retain their interest in the lesson. For the teacher with five different classes in one day, it is also useful to be able to recall previous class notes with one click.

- Individualized learning plans allow pupils to work in appropriate groupings using a variety of software packages (for example Sibelius, Logic Audio, Rave E Jay and GuitarCoach).

- Monitoring sheets are held by staff and pupils to keep track of each pupil's progress and ensure the quality of each pupil's learning.

Ongoing plans and into the future

At King's Park we have already begun making links with other countries to expand the expertise available to our students online. One member of the team has begun developing the sound engineering facility in the department. With an increasing number of pupils choosing to study this area of the music curriculum, facilities are currently being reviewed. We look forward to adding more of the latest music technology available when budgets allow.

We were also delighted to assist the music development officer for Glasgow in promoting the latest ICT music initiatives to other Glasgow teachers.

Aileen Monaghan

Chapter 8

Leadership for personalization

John West-Burnham

This chapter explores the issues and implications of moving towards personalizing learning. It would be profoundly wrong to underestimate the impact of personalization on schools. As the previous sections in this book have demonstrated, personalizing learning calls into question a host of assumptions about the way in which schools work – most obviously:

- the knowledge base and professional practice of teachers;

- the principles underpinning school design and organization;

- the role of pupils and students;

- the nature of the curriculum;

- the criteria for effectiveness.

The extent of the change is powerfully demonstrated by Hargreaves (2004) in his discussion of 'educational imaginary' – the unquestioned assumptions that we make about the social and moral nature of our society. He draws a distinction between the educational imaginaries of the nineteenth and twenty-first centuries and these have been summarized in Table 8.1. Hargreaves concludes his discussion:

> *Personalizing learning ... may be seen as the driver from the 19th century educational imaginary to that of the 21st century ... The evolution of educational imaginaries is now so fast that the same leaders live through the transition and have to lead and manage it. It is this that makes the leadership of personalizing learning so important and so challenging.* (Hargreaves, 2004: page 32)

It is relatively easy to conceptualize a new educational imaginary – the real challenge is to convert it into changed beliefs, attitudes and practice.

Not least of the problems is that many of those who will have to change are the successful products of the nineteenth-century educational imaginary. It is much more than the status quo, it is their personal history, their success and, for many, the source of their personal and professional identity. Two apparently contradictory factors operate in this context: it is highly unlikely that personalizing learning would ever be the subject of legislation. It is more likely to be the result of advice and exhortation and it will only really work at the level of professional practice and school culture. However, there are a significant number of school leaders and educationalists that have a substantial and highly successful experience of personalizing learning – those who work in special schools. The best practice in special education has used the following strategies for many years:

- personal learning plans

- negotiated pathways through the curriculum

- specially selected learning resources

- high levels of social and community interaction

- use of each student's preferred learning style.

Table 8.1 Educational 'imaginaries' (after Hargreaves, 2004: pages 30–32)

Nineteenth-century educational imaginary	Twenty-first century educational imaginary
Students are prepared for a fixed situation in life	Students' identities and destinations are fluid
Intelligence is fixed	Intelligence is multidimensional
Schools are culturally homogeneous	Schools are heterogeneous
Schools of a type are interchangeable	Schools of a type are diverse
Schooling is limited for the majority	Schooling provides personalized learning for all
Schools have rigid and clear boundaries	Education is lifelong for every student
Schools work on the factory model	Education is unconstrained by time and place
Roles are sharply defined and segregated	Roles are blurred and overlapping
Schools and teachers work autonomously	Schools and educators work in complex networks
Education is producer led	Education is user led

It might well be that one of the most powerful strategies to support personalization would be for more schools and teachers to learn from practice in special needs education.

There is one other broad area of principle that may be worth exploring to support implementation of personalizing learning. It would seem highly unreasonable to expect teachers to work in a culture of like this if they have not experienced personalization for themselves. There are several ways in which this might be done:

- Increasing the levels of choice over the content and mode of CPD.

- Greater negotiation over deployment and teaching loads.

- Providing opportunities for the delivery of programmes outside the teachers' normal workload.

- Using opportunities created by the remodelling programme to allow teachers to focus their time and energy on learning and teaching.

As a school moves towards personalizing learning then all adults in the school need to be involved, in personal terms, with the design and development of the actual experience of learning. It would be impossible to move straight from Hargreaves' nineteenth-century imaginary to full personalization – it will have to be an incremental process.

This chapter will explore the movement towards personalizing learning by focusing on the following aspects of leadership:

- learning-centred leadership

- trust

- leadership styles

- leadership for change.

Learning-centred leadership

It seems axiomatic to argue that the personalization of learning depends on learning-centred leadership. But this in fact raises a fundamental issue – personalization is not just about incremental improvements in teaching, delivering the curriculum or raising standards. Personalizing learning is about a fundamental change in the philosophy and culture of schools. If it is to be embedded in practice and lead to sustained change, then it requires an equivalent change in leadership strategies and behaviour.

Learning-centred leadership is emerging as one of the most coherent ways of describing the leadership behaviours that are most likely to move a school towards being a learning community. In the broadest terms, learning-centred leaders have the following characteristics:

- Personal values that focus on the effective learning, success and achievement of every individual.

- A coherent and systematic understanding of learning that informs all aspects of their work as leaders.

- The ability to engage in structured dialogue to enhance the understanding of learning in others.

- A commitment to supporting the learning of others.

- A public demonstration of his or her own engagement in learning.

- A joy in the success, growth and achievement of all.

This set of criteria is a long way from the management duties of the curriculum deputy in the secondary school 20 years ago. Learning-centred leadership is fundamental to personalization because the two factors are entwined. Without learning-centred leadership personalization could be reduced to a series of strategies to reinforce effective teaching.

Southworth (2004) has identified three strategies that leaders can use to influence the quality of learning in schools: modelling, monitoring and dialogue. As is shown in Figure 8.1, these elements are closely interrelated. The strategy of mentoring has been added as the unifying force that allows optimum expression of the other three.

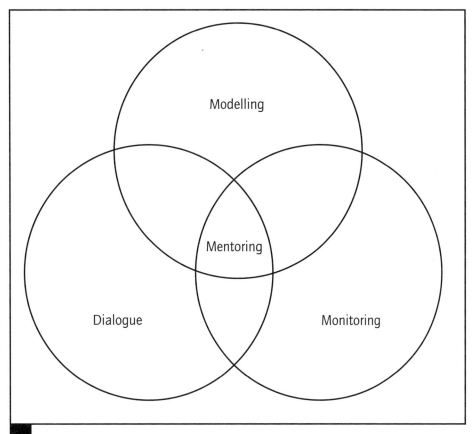

Figure 8.1 Strategies for learning-centred leadership (after Southworth, 2004)

Southworth defines the three elements in the following terms:

Modelling
Modelling is concerned with the power of example. Teachers and headteachers believe in setting an example because they know this influences pupils and colleagues alike. Research shows that teachers watch their leaders closely. And teachers watch what their leaders do in order to check if leaders' actions are consistent over time and to test whether leaders do as they say. Teachers do not follow leaders who cannot 'walk the talk'. (page 6)

Monitoring

Monitoring includes analysing and acting on pupil progress and outcome data (for example, assessment and test scores, evaluation data, school performance trends, parental opinion surveys, pupil attendance data, pupil interview information). Leadership is stronger and more effective when it is informed by data on pupils' learning, progress and achievements as well as by direct knowledge of all teaching practices and classroom dynamics. (page 7)

Dialogue

Dialogue in this context is about creating opportunities for teachers to talk with their colleagues about learning and teaching. The kinds of dialogues which influence what happens in classrooms are focused on learning and teaching. Leaders create the circumstances to meet with colleagues and discuss pedagogy and pupil learning. (page 8)

Mentoring with coaching provides one of the most significant strategies for leaders to support the development of colleagues. As Goleman (2002) expresses it:

Coaching's surprisingly positive emotional impact stems largely from the empathy and rapport a leader establishes with employees. A good coach communicates a belief in people's potentials and an expectation that they can do their best. The tacit message is, 'I believe in you, I'm investing in you, and I expect your best efforts'. As a result, people sense that the leader cares, so they feel motivated to uphold their own high standards for performance, and they feel accountable for how well they do. (page 62)

The combination of these four strategies forms a powerful nexus that has the potential to:

- personalize leadership engagement with colleagues;

- form a model practice of the most effective relationships with learners;

- demonstrate high-profile consistent commitment to the core purpose of the school.

For Sergiovanni (2001):

Learning earns the centre-stage position because it is a powerful way for schools to adapt, to stay ahead, and to invent new solutions. At the heart of any successful change is a change in culture which makes new goals, new initiatives, and new ways of behaving part of a school's norm structure. ... Though we have no inventory of scientific findings to present, it seems clear that we can be much more deliberate in organizing schools in ways that enhance teacher learning and the learning of other adults. (page 119)

Learning-centred leadership is fundamental to personalization, if for no other reason than that personalization, in order to work, has to be the direct expression of a school refocusing itself on the learning of the individual. It would be wrong to underestimate the challenge of moving from managing an externally imposed curriculum, in order to raise standards, to leading learning in order to maximize the achievement of all members of the school community.

Trust

It is difficult to imagine one single factor that is as important to the successful implementation of personalization as trust. The extent to which leaders create a climate of trust is a key determinant of the potential success of personalization as trust, to a substantial degree, decides the status of the individual. For O'Neill (2002) trust is a fundamental requirement for any society or organization:

> Confucius told his disciple Tzu-kung that three things are needed for government: weapons, food and trust. If a ruler can't hold on to all three, he should give up the weapons first and the food next. Trust should be guarded to the end: without trust we cannot stand. (page 3)

> It isn't only rulers and governments who prize and need trust. Each of us and every profession and every institution need trust. We need it because we have to be able to rely on others acting as they say that they will, and because we need others to accept that we will as we say we will. The sociologist Niklas Luhmann was right that 'A complete absence of trust would prevent [one] even getting up in the morning.' (pages 3–4)

Bryk and Schneider (2002) provide a detailed and systematic analysis of the nature and place of trust in schools.

> A complex web of social exchanges conditions the basic operations of schools. Embedded in the daily social routines of schools is an interrelated set of mutual dependencies among all key actors: students, teachers, principals and administrators, and parents. (page 20)

> Relational trust views the social exchanges of schooling as organized around a distinct set of role relationships: teachers with students, teachers with other teachers, teachers with parents and with their school principal. Each party in a role relationship maintains an understanding of his or her role obligations and holds some expectations about the role of the other. (page 20)

> Relational trust, so conceived, is appropriately viewed as an organizational property in that its constitutive elements are socially defined in the reciprocal exchanges among participants in a school community, and its presence (or absence) has important consequences for the functioning of the school and its capacity to engage in fundamental change. (page 22)

For Bryk and Schneider relational trust is the basis for understanding personal relationships, organizational relationships as expressed in roles and responsibilities and organizational culture as the collective capacity of the school to act collaboratively. They have no doubt as to the central importance and impact of trust on schools:

> First, collective decision making with broad teacher buy-in occurs more readily in schools with strong relational trust.

> Second, when relational trust is strong, reform initiatives are more likely to be deeply engaged by school participants and to defuse broadly across the organization.

Third, relational trust forments a moral imperative to take on the hard work of school improvement. Teachers had a full-time job prior to reform. Most worked hard at their teaching, doing the best they could for as many students as they could. In addition to taking risks with new classroom practices, reform also requires teachers to take on extra work: for example, engaging with colleagues in planning, implementing, and evaluating school improvement initiatives. (Bryk and Schneider, 2002: pages 122–123)

Bryk and Schneider stress the importance of social exchanges, role relationships and role obligations. These factors are often expressed by schools in terms of organizational structures and the pivotal nature of the extent to which authority is shared. In this context authority is best defined as:

If individuals are to bring their strivings and passions to their work (as their bosses desperately want), they must now rely more on internalized images of themselves – on an emotional appreciation of who they are, who they wish to become and what they can contribute specifically to an enterprise. They have to rely in greater measure on their own personal authority. (Hirschhorn, 1997: page 9, emphasis in the original)

The level to which authority is monopolized or shared is a direct manifestation of the degree to which leadership is the personal status of an individual or a collective capacity within the school. In this context trust is perhaps best understood in the way that it is expressed in families with the changing relationship between parents and their children. As the trust that parents have in their children grows with age, maturity and confidence, so the transactional nature of their relationship changes, for example:

- there is less permission seeking and giving;
- decisions are increasingly delegated, in other words choices are left to the child;
- the demand for detailed accountability diminishes (usually to avoid mutual embarrassment);
- the amount of negotiation increases.

In essence, the relationship changes from immature control to mature trust; as with the family so possibly with the school. The model of learning proposed in Figure 3.1 links the movement from shallow to deep and profound learning, to the movement from dependency through interdependency to independence. As understood in this book, personalizing learning is the process of developing mature, autonomous and self-reliant learners.

The nature of this changing relationship can be fully explored in Figure 8.2.

| CONTROL | DELEGATION | EMPOWERMENT | SUBSIDIARITY |

Low trust	High trust
Immature	Mature
Dependency	Independence

Figure 8.2 Trust and organizational relationships

In Figure 8.2, as organizational relationships move across the spectrum from left to right so the level of trust increases. In the first category relationships are characterized by control, a hierarchical 'chain of command' model in which superordinates define the choices of subordinates. This is the classic hierarchical model, having power located with an individual who operates in a transactional manner. This approach can be justified in extreme circumstances – an emergency, when a person is in danger and so on. However, it is a denial of the individual and, in its most extreme expression, creates dependency and compliance. It would be inappropriate to draw too strong a parallel between totalitarian models of leadership and some classrooms, but the lack of personal choice, the imposition of activities and the dominance of one person's values and perspectives can create a sense of helplessness and subordination. This has to be the ultimate denial of personalization – it not only diminishes the person, it also denies the possibility of the development of personal potential.

Most organizations, not least schools, have long recognized the inhibiting nature of hierarchical control. The sheer complexity of modern organizations makes individual rule practically impossible. Therefore, most schools have, of necessity, moved to a model of delegation that is best understood as a balance of authority and responsibility. In essence both are delegated but in very different permutations and ratios. Thus a high level of responsibility may not be matched by commensurate authority. This may well be one of the most significant weaknesses in the design of schools as organizations and a major cause of discontent – the failure to provide sufficient authority to discharge a specific responsibility. It therefore becomes a modified form of control – a permission-seeking and permission-giving culture. Delegation can be a powerful exemplification of trust if responsibility and authority are in balance – an imbalance is inevitably dysfunctional unless defined within a developmental context with a clear strategy to enhance authority as knowledge, skills, experience and maturity grow.

Empowerment is delegation without caveat, where authority is sufficient to or greater than the level needed to meet the demands of the responsibility agreed. In many ways empowerment has echoes of double-loop learning; it is the ability to initiate and modify strategies without recourse to 'asking permission'. Empowerment is about the agreement of ends and discretion over means; it recognizes and respects personal autonomy and ability, irrespective of age or status.

This respect is taken to its ultimate expression in the concept of subsidiarity, introduced by Charles Handy (1994):

> Subsidiarity, however, depends on a mutual confidence. Those in the centre have to have confidence in the unit, while the unit has to have confidence in the centre and the members of the unit have to have confidence in each other. When the mutual confidence exists, there is no need for the books of procedures, the manuals, inspectors, performance numbers and counter-signatures which clutter up large organizations. These are all the signs of distrust, the atmosphere of fear which makes so many organizations seem like prisons for the human soul. They should not, need not, be like that. Our work can be our pride. Put it this way: we want to be able to sign our own work. (pages 122–123)

Subsidiarity is probably best understood as federalism – a balance between shared consent about certain overarching principles and local autonomy where centralization is not appropriate – a classic example would be the education system in Australia which is developed and operated by each state in a distinctive way. In the case of schools it might be expressed in a highly autonomous early years' unit in a primary school or a largely autonomous faculty in a secondary school.

Subsidiarity is not about the ultimate expression of individualism, it is about achieving a balance that reconciles the need for organizational coherence and consistency with optimum levels of choice and self-direction. The continuum from control to subsidiarity can also be seen as a movement from crude and simplistic answerability to a reciprocal moral accountability.

The importance of this analysis of the relationship between organizational design, culture and trust lies in the idea that the dominant mode of the organization as a whole will determine how its constituents function. Thus, if a school management team works in a high-responsibility, low-authority mode then that might be seen as the most significant factor in how teams work and so how classrooms operate. This is a graphic illustration of the importance of modelling. For personalization to really work, school leadership will have to create a culture at the macro level that informs the mezzo level of the team and the micro level of the classroom. Another way to think of this is as a fractal relationship:

> *And I believe that fractals also have direct application for the leadership of organizations. The very best organizations have a fractal quality to them. An observer of such an organization can tell what the organization's values and ways of doing business are by watching anyone, whether it be a production floor employee or a senior manager. There is a consistency and predictability to the quality of behaviour. No matter where we look in these organizations, self-similarity is found in its people, in spite of the complex range of roles and levels.*
> (Wheatley, 1992: page 132)

Trust is axiomatic to personalization – without it the individual cannot grow and trust; by definition, it is a direct function of leadership choices, structures and styles.

Leadership styles

In one of his most powerful phrases Goleman (2002) argues that:

 When leaders operate with dissonant styles, the resulting culture is inevitably toxic. (page 194)

Leadership for learning-centredness and, so, personalization has to recognize that leadership behaviour has a disproportionately significant impact on organizational culture and climate. Therefore, if the personalization of learning is to be embedded in school cultures there are real implications for the dominant and consistent modes of behaviour for leaders at school, team and classroom level.

Goleman (2002: page 55) identifies six styles that are available to leaders, summarized here as:

VISIONARY:

Moves people towards shared dreams and values
Most strongly positive impact on climate

COACHING:

Focuses on individual capability and engagement
Highly positive impact on climate

AFFILIATIVE:

Builds networks and personal relationships
Positive impact on climate

DEMOCRATIC:

Secures engagement through participation
Positive impact on climate

PACESETTING:

Sets challenging goals
Often highly negative impact on climate

COMMANDING:

'Do it because I say so'
Often highly negative impact on climate

If personalization is to become the norm by which schools operate then the appropriate leadership style, or combination of styles, is clearly a powerful initiating and sustaining factor. There are direct links to be made between Goleman's descriptions of the least effective styles and the model of trust in schools developed in Figure 8.2. Authoritative leadership is about securing commitment rather than compliance, while coaching is about building capacity and enabling the individual – both of these factors explicitly and implicitly reinforce the principles of learning centredness and personalizing learning. If leadership is a collective capacity rather than personal status, then what has been written above applies to everyone in a school who has any responsibility for the effective learning of others.

Leadership for change

One of the great oxymorons is the notion that it is possible to manage change. By definition, change is so complex and involves so many fundamental questions that it has to involve leadership. It also needs management – but only in the sense of consolidating and sustaining change.

Personalizing learning has the potential to call into question virtually every assumption that currently exists about schools and schooling. It might well be that the process of implementing the personalization of learning not only changes the educational imaginary (in Hargreaves' terms), but also in doing so will require school leaders to preside over the most radical questioning of the schooling system ever seen.

One of the first issues to be considered is the extent of personalization to be undertaken. Figure 8.3 explores the possible phases of personalizing learning – the issue for those leading the implementation of an innovation is just how much change is actually required.

SHALLOW

- Predominantly teacher control of lesson content and teaching strategies

- Limited reference to learning styles

- Homogeneous cohort progression

- Some use of study skills

- Largely summative assessment

- Random/ad hoc personal support and advice

- ICT to reinforce teaching

DEEP

- Some degree of negotiation over lesson content and teaching and learning strategies

- Recognition of learning styles

- Some opportunity for individual pathways

- Structured use of thinking strategies

- Some negotiated formative assessment

- Limited personal mentoring/coaching

- ICT to support personal learning programmes

PROFOUND

- Student direction (with advice) over curriculum content and learning strategies

- Strong focus on learning styles in the design of learning activities

- Largely personalized individual pathways

- Cognitive intervention strategies

- Negotiated assessment

- Mentoring and coaching as an entitlement

- ICT to manage personalization

Figure 8.3 Phases of personalizing learning

Figure 8.3 gives an artificial sense of coherence and linearity. The reality is much more likely to be incremental with different aspects of personalization being adapted at different times and in a piecemeal way.

For some schools the movement to shallow personalization may represent such a challenge as to be as much as they might reasonably be expected to accomplish given their history, stakeholder perceptions and expectations and their perceived core purpose. For other schools, for ideological or totally pragmatic reasons, the movement to deep or profound implementation of personalization may be the most appropriate way forward.

Whatever the depth of innovation decided on, it would seem that a range of factors need to be in place in order to ensure that personalizing learning becomes the dominant paradigm informing school practice rather than a series of minor and optional adjustments to existing practice. Schools, like most organizations, have a remarkable capacity to assimilate, modify, adapt, compromise and, if necessary, ignore externally imposed innovation. The success or otherwise of personalizing learning will be the result of:

1. Restating values: personalization might represent such a fundamental realignment of the values of some schools, school leaders and teachers that it may be necessary to focus on fundamental principles and initiate a debate in the school which focuses on:

   ● equity, entitlement and inclusion

   ● the role and purpose of education

   ● the nature of the educated person

   ● the science of learning

   ● the role of the teacher.

   In practical terms this would mean a reconsideration of the school's aims and values, review of its perceived core purpose and redefinition of core roles, and so on.

2. Building shared understanding: this is where Southworth's concept of dialogue (2004: pages 101–102) and Goleman's models of authoritative leadership and coaching are so important. It is in the building of shared understanding through conversations built on a common vocabulary that informed commitment is most likely to be achieved. This implies that leadership develops a shared mental model of personalizing learning that is then used in a consistent way to inform a wide range of discussions, conversations and debates.

3. Building capacity: the successful implementation of personalizing learning will require some significant additions to or redirection of the skills found in schools, for example:

   ● mentoring and coaching

   ● negotiating learning pathways and outcomes

   ● understanding learning styles and teaching strategies

   ● interpersonal skills and collaborative strategies

   ● monitoring, review, reflection and evaluation.

In the final analysis, change is a learning process – the implementation of personalization has to model effective learning and recognize that organizations do not change – the people in them do. Coming to terms with the profound changes that personalization involves means that individuals have to internalize a new way of thinking about themselves and their organizations. The potential of any individual to change can be seen as the result of a complex interaction between his or her readiness and capability.

Readiness: the extent to which individuals are engaged, motivated and committed to the school's vision and values, and are working with energy and enthusiasm.

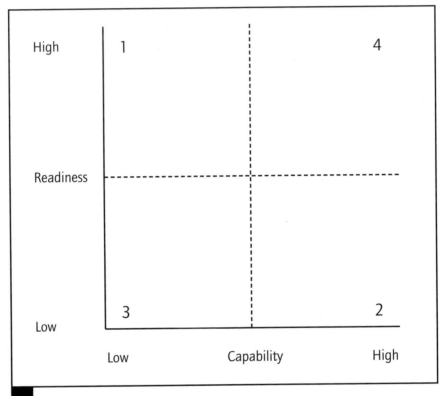

Figure 8.4 Readiness and capability (after Everard and Morris, 1996: page 243)

Capability: the levels of knowledge, skills, personal resources and authority that individuals bring to the school (Everard and Morris, 1996: page 243).

1. **High readiness – Low capability**
   Very positive and enthusiastic but limited knowledge and expertise.

2. **High capability – Low readiness**
   Very experienced with high knowledge and skills but lacking motivation
   and engagement.

3. **Low capability – Low readiness**
   Very limited motivation and engagement, limited skills and knowledge –
   no authority.

4. **High capability -- High readiness**
   A combination of high engagement and commitment with knowledge, skills
   and authority.

The extent to which a school can approach change, development and improvement with confidence is directly related to the level of 'fourness'; the greater the number of staff in the top right-hand quadrant of the model shown in Figure 8.4, the greater the levels of capacity, resilience and sustainability available to the school.

The model can be used to explore the potential effectiveness of a leadership team, any group or project team, or the whole staff. Having located individuals on the model it is then important to move people from quadrants 1, 2 and 3.

In general terms:

- Moving people from quadrant 1 to 4 is about learning and development – the leader as coach.

- Moving people from quadrant 2 to 4 is about motivation and engagement – authoritative leadership.

- Moving people from quadrant 3 to 4 is highly complex and difficult, and may even be counterproductive in terms of leadership energy and time.

- Sustaining people in quadrant 4 is a central leadership responsibility.

Even for those who are fully committed, confident and capable, change represents a fundamental challenge. The process of implementing personalization holds many uncertainties. Capra (2002) captures the contradictions and tensions perfectly:

> *The experience of the critical instability that precedes the emergence of novelty may involve uncertainty, fear, confusion or self doubt. Experienced leaders recognize these emotions as integral parts of the whole dynamic and create a climate of trust and mutual support.*

> *During the change process some of the old structures may fall apart, but if the supportive climate and the feedback loops in the network of communications persist, new and more meaningful structures are likely to emerge. When that happens, people often feel a sense of wonder and elation, and now the leader's role is to acknowledge these emotions and provide opportunities for celebration.*
> (page 108)

Case Studies

Chapter 9

Creating a climate for learning

Headteacher: Hazel Pulley

Caldecote Community Primary School, Leicester

Is it the application of theory that helps us to lead the way or is it the fusion of experience with knowledge that provides the road map? Maybe it is simply integrity and reflective experience that shapes leadership. If it is the latter then surely the leader in question must display a critical mass of emotional intelligence taking others with them through the kind of effective interpersonal engagement that is described in John West-Burnham's paper, *Interpersonal Leadership* (2002).

The inscription 'know thyself', written in the Temple of Apollo at Delphi, is extended by West-Burnham to 'know thyself, know thy others, then act'. But is that enough?

When appointed to lead my present school I applied the extended 'know thyself' to an agreed vision for our new school; a vision that involved using emotional intelligence to improve relationships and academic achievement.

Setting foundations – a leadership story

I was appointed early one term to work with two schools that were to amalgamate the following term. These were two schools that demonstrated immense diversity of attitude, purpose and, most of all, vision. As headteacher designate, I spent most of the pre-term working among everyone in the new school community, moving us all to a shared vision and creating a raft or emotional climate that would carry all staff and pupils together through a sea of unknown calms and storms. To create this climate, the vision was explored and manifested into values which all agreed would help lead our actions and decisions within school. Moving the values into actions required me to be highly self-aware and allow the knowledge of my emotions and personal values to become symbiotic with my leadership style and leadership being.

Vision into values

Through moving the school vision into explicit values, opportunities for children to become aware of their emotional reactions and how they interacted with others were provided.

Therefore, including emotional literacy in the school curriculum and behaviour policy had a real impact on pupils' behaviour.

Darren flopped on the easy chair in my office, appearing quite at ease. This was a boy who had presented challenging behaviour throughout Years 5 and 6, for as long as I had known him since becoming headteacher at Caldecote Community Primary School. Darren used to arrive in turmoil in the morning in deep sombre moods, refusing to work and hating the world, determined not to learn or become a sociable member of his class. I asked him how he was feeling as his transition to high school approached at the end of the week. 'I okay – I understand my feelings', was the shining reply, a reply that was confirmed with a confident look.

This is one of those moments that teachers treasure. Darren appeared to be aware of his emotional reactions. Darren had become self-aware, or at least appeared well on his way to being in a state of self-awareness.

In our school, self-awareness is nurtured within our pupils through the high profile we give to emotional intelligence. Opportunities for children to explore their emotional awareness were placed within our curriculum delivery, and strategies were designed to encourage children to reflect upon their behaviour and that of others.

Our school values referenced the way forward and our supportive acronym ADA (attitudes, demeanours and approaches) helps staff approach its whole work with emotional intelligence, not just for pupils but for the whole school. Our deputy head and PHSE (personal health and social education) co-ordinator designed a whole new curriculum, with PHSE as the spine, circle time (a structured discussion of significant issues) and Philosophy for Children (P4C) sessions given spots in the timetable.

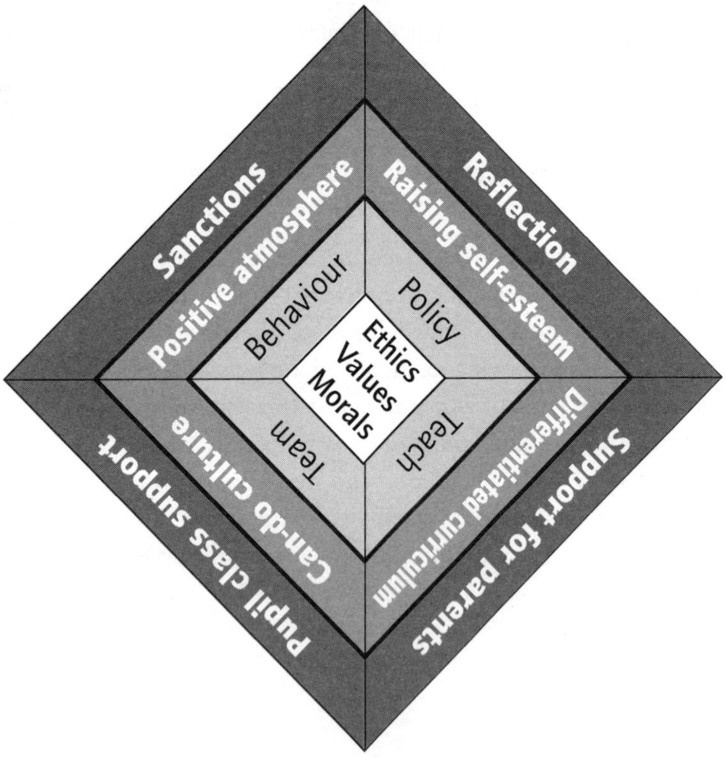

Time for reflection

The behaviour management diamond (see Figure 9.1) provides many opportunities for 'emotional lessons' facilitated by the behaviour mentor primarily but also by all the staff in school. The behaviour mentor is a member of staff with specific responsibility for supporting the emotional intelligence strategies.

Figure 9.1 Caldecote Community Primary School behaviour management

Particular elements within the diamond design provide specific opportunities for pupils to understand their emotions, for example the usage of time-out cards by pupils and staff. Time-out cards indicate that a pupil needs time away from the classroom. The cards specify either five or ten minutes, and we are looking at introducing 20 minutes cards shortly. A pupil may be issued with a time-out card by his or her teacher or he or she may choose to issue one him or herself. By using a time-out card a pupil is able to indicate that he or she needs time-out away from the classroom for calming and reflection.

By using these cards important choices are encouraged by pupils and staff. By leaving the classroom and sitting with the behaviour mentor for the requisite time, pupils have guided time to reflect on moods, reactions or recently displayed behaviours. The behaviour mentor helps the pupils to understand these feelings and impulsive reactions, building a path for the pupil towards self-awareness.

When the time is up the pupil should be ready to return. The staff member in the classroom greets the child on his or her return, showing pleasure that the child has changed his or her behaviour and that all are ready to move on. These cards are well used by both pupils and staff and children are praised for using them, and for choosing how long out they need, rather than storming off, kicking furniture or, even worse, hurting themselves or others.

Using 'chances'

Each day children in our school have six chances to make the right choice, moving away from a wrong choice. Following a first verbal warning, a card is issued if behaviour does not improve. These cards act as a prompt to children, encouraging them to look at their behaviour/mood and ask for help to understand it or to change it themselves. If they continue to use up their 'chances' their names are underlined and help sought for them by the member of staff. This may necessitate the behaviour mentor being called to class, at the same time as issuing a time-out card. At all times the pupil is praised where the right choice is made.

Through conducting classroom-context questionnaires we have carefully monitored how children in our school view our emotionally intelligent climate. Through circle time, school council and P4C we are able to provide the children with a time where they feel listened to and valued. Fairness is also a strong feature of our work and there is intense weekly monitoring of rewards and sanctions per pupil and class. In a large primary school, it is often a dilemma for the headteacher when implementing initiatives as to how fairly and cohesively they are used and delivered by staff in the school environment. Regular monitoring ensures fairness, and results are displayed on a special board in the corridor for pupils, parents and staff to view.

The presence of a nurture group (Sealife Room) within our school provides a context from where emotional intelligence flows. The Sealife Room accommodates 12 Key Stage 1 children for 3½ days of the week, allowing the room to be used by the rest of the school for another two sessions enabling co-operative behaviour to be promoted through specific play activities. A focus on raising self-esteem is also a strong feature of this room within our school.

And back to the temple ...

Understanding emotions and relating behaviours to feelings is now paramount in our school. Developing interpersonal skills between staff and pupils, although not without the odd squall at sea, has created a climate of respect and understanding. There have been many challenging moments that tested and rattled the vision and values of the new school, for example managed moves of children into our school following exclusion from others. My own self-awareness and moral confidence enabled me to model our values into practice and also gather more onto the raft. Monitoring staff approaches, demeanours and attitudes within a culture of respect paid dividends and quickly enhanced good practice.

There is a real sense that we are making progress, but we are still committed to developing a better understanding of the process that we are engaged in. There are many questions still to be answered.

So is it 'knowing thyself' that enables a leader to implement vision into practice or is it much more? What enables leaders, teachers and pupils to get on board? Is it the ease of ingress or the compelling shape and comfort of the raft that is appealing? Is there a defined process that enables leaders to weather the storms? Does an experience, such as amalgamation, create much new? Did knowledge of theory support the vision?

Chapter 10

Philosophy of education: a holistic curriculum

Principal: Ian McKenzie

Kambrya College, Berwick, Victoria, Australia

Developing students within a holistic world context is central to both what we teach and how we teach at Kambrya College. Our students' future is being shaped by factors that are peculiar to the age we live in and the future we are moving towards. There are three main areas that we consider are going to be the major ones for changes to the world context in the future.

Technology

The future we are preparing our students for has largely not been invented yet. The nature and type of employment our students will be asked to do will be completely different from that we see today. We are preparing students to live and work within a society that does not yet exist. As a result of this, education can no longer be seen as the giver of public information. With the enormous amount of information made available, largely by technology, how could we ever decide which piece of information a student will need to remember over another? Schooling needs to be seen as a way for students to gain the necessary skills to continue learning throughout their lives, not seen as an end in itself.

Environment

Our actions today will become major environmental problems in our students' futures. We first need to develop awareness in students of the problems and, second, we need to give students the necessary skills to provide some long-term solutions that will lead to a sustainable future. Traditionally we have taught students to break the world up into segments and, as a result, the big picture has been lost. Students need to learn to appreciate the interrelated context that exists. How can we expect students to solve a problem like the 'greenhouse effect' if students only understand scientifically why the problem occurs, without also seeing the implications of social issues, political agendas and economic rationalization? The problems we face are big problems that cannot be solved by just breaking them down into smaller problems.

Relationships

The human values we live by are as valid today as they will be in our students' futures. Treating others with the same rights and privileges as we would wish for ourselves is timeless. What has changed, and will continue to change, is the modern context that human interaction takes place in and the pressures this places on human relationships. Technology has meant that we can now communicate and relate to people in many different ways. We can form relationships with people across the other side of the world without ever having any personal contact; we are a truly global society. If we look at the development in communications over the last 20 years and then attempt to peer 20 years ahead, the world of science fiction may give us our best glimpse as to what may exist. Living in a global society is both a challenge and an adventure which our students need to prepare for.

Developing students for the new millennium

With the vision of developing a curriculum, which will prepare our students for the future, we have come up with six broad, essential outcomes that we believe our students need to develop in order for them to become members of society who can thrive within a global context. For students to improve in these areas they will need to grow and develop from a range of learning experiences that are presented to them. These learning experiences are available as part of an integrated curriculum that emphasizes a holistic context rather than separating learning into neat, yet artificial, subject packages. Within this integrated curriculum, students are involved in learning activities not confined to traditional subjects, with the focus on developing skills and knowledge that can be transferred to a range of circumstances. This vision of developing whole students who see themselves and their learning within a bigger context is shown in the model for what we teach at Kambrya College (Figure 10.1).

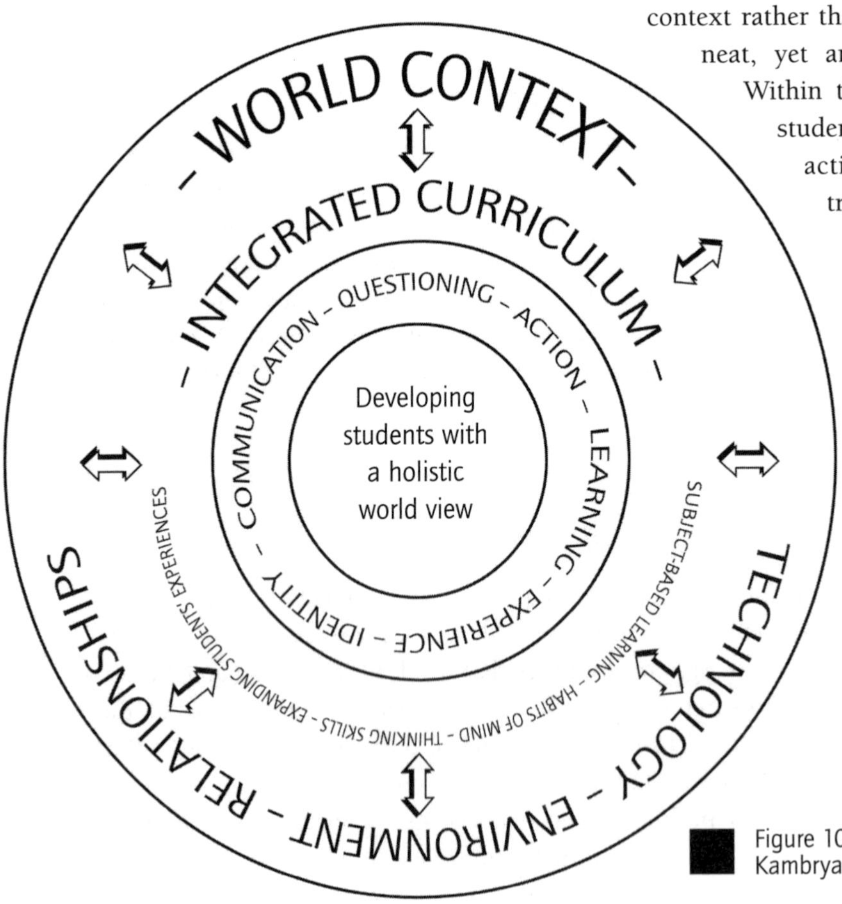

Figure 10.1 Curriculum model at Kambrya College

Teaching and learning

Student centred

Kambrya College has a student-centred approach to teaching and learning. This recognizes that students learn by constructing their own personal views of concepts and link these to previous experiences unique to each individual. This individually constructed meaning is formed only after passing through each person's values, belief system and cultural background.

With this constructivist view of education, the traditional view of teaching and learning that focused on presenting isolated pieces of information can only be seen as ineffective. Instead we focus on students developing their own belief systems and views of the world by presenting a variety of learning experiences for them to learn within. Ongoing reflection by both teachers and students is the mechanism for optimizing teaching and learning at Kambrya College.

Teaching and learning are seen as continual processes of design, act, reflection and redesign. To help in this process, teachers at Kambrya College are active participants of PEEL (Project Enhancing Effective Learning). PEEL gives teachers a forum to reflect on student learning and how it can be improved. As a result, teaching strategies are designed to address the dynamic needs of students within the classroom.

There is a strong focus at Kambrya College on students developing transferable skills in their learning and also on developing positive learning habits. This focus will enable students to become lifelong learners who are able to adapt and change throughout life. The direct teaching of thinking skills is particularly important in development as a lifelong learner. Students learn techniques and strategies to help them effectively think in a number of different ways. Techniques in critical thinking, constructive thinking, creative (lateral) thinking and parallel thinking are taught directly at Kambrya. Students are then encouraged to practise applying these to appropriate situations throughout the curriculum. Another focus for teaching and learning in the school is students working effectively in small groups to help each other achieve their best. Based on the 'team small group' model, students take on roles within a group to help others in their learning while also developing interpersonal and group-work skills.

Essential outcomes

At Kambrya College our students work towards the six outcomes below. By working towards these our students will be empowered to survive and prosper in an ever-changing world by continuing to learn and adapt to the experiences and challenges that they encounter.

Identity

To develop an awareness and confidence in our identities as individuals, as members of the local community, as Australians and as global citizens.

Through developing awareness and understanding of their own unique identity and talents, students are able to gain confidence in themselves and acceptance and tolerance of others. We then expand this view to a community, national and international perspective, and explore how all these unique individuals work together to form our local, national and global community. With this expanding view, students are able to start discovering possibilities and visions for their own futures.

Action

To develop the self-belief to take action so we can bring about positive change in ourselves, in our community, in our country and globally.

Students are encouraged to take positive risks, to put their ideas into practice, to play a sport they would not normally play, to articulate their concerns, to contribute to class discussions, to speak out against peers when they believe they are wrong, to play music, to act, to join a club, to sing and to dance. Action is the goal of all our curricular and extra-curricular activities. We understand that students acting on their own ideas are dependent on belief in themselves. This belief is best developed in an environment that does not just recognize the 'right answer' as its goal, but promotes taking action and contributing to the school community as its primary concern.

Learning

To become self-sufficient and self-motivated lifelong learners.

Reflection is the key to students becoming lifelong learners. Students and teachers reflect on how they learn best. Through reflecting we develop skills and behaviours that help us to become good learners now and in the future. Learning to think in different ways, to develop a broad perspective before making a decision, to think creatively when solving problems and to organize our thinking, are what we focus on achieving in this outcome.

Communication

To develop the skills and the confidence to communicate our ideas about the world to others in a variety of ways and to recognize the right that we all have to convey our message.

In this technological age the amount of information and means to communicate this information have expanded beyond traditional ways. Students will develop skills in acquiring, sorting and presenting information and then communicating this to others in an appropriate way. With this development students will communicate their ideas about the world. This personal voice may take a more traditional form, such as writing, speaking, dancing, drawing, painting, sculpting and singing, or it may make use of new technology, or any combination of these.

Questioning

To be able to observe, describe, analyse and create our own view of the world.

Students need to be able to observe and analyse in detail the information they receive. This is done so that students are able to form a personal view of the world by developing their own values rather than blindly accepting the information of others. This will involve students critically examining the information they receive and deciding for themselves the relevance and validity of that information.

Experience

We seek to continually expand our field of experience so we can adapt, learn and grow in an ever-changing world.

We recognize that students need to expand their circle of experience. It is when students are put in new situations that they are challenged, grow and learn. We continually provide students with challenges and new experiences. We expect students to grasp these challenges with both hands, to contribute and participate in them to their full potential and so learn from these experiences.

Chapter 11

Creating a learning-centred school

Headteacher: Greg Barker

St Vincent's Catholic Primary School, Warrington, Cheshire

A policy for teaching for learning

The aims expressed in our Mission Statement significantly influence and guide our teaching for learning policy. These aims are:

1. *To create for each individual a working partnership between home, parish and school and to foster close relationships with the wider community.*

2. *To foster happy, caring relationships within a school which offers a safe and secure environment and enables individuals to grow in confidence, dignity and self-esteem.*

3. *To provide a broad and balanced curriculum in a Catholic setting, in which each child grows in knowledge and understanding through the acquisition of skills, attitudes and values, and so enabling them to become active contributors to society.*

4. *To make prayer, worship and liturgy real educational experiences in nurturing the faith development of each individual.*

The above aims feed into the specific aims of this policy, which are to:

- continuously improve the quality of teaching and learning experiences offered to our pupils;

- give children the opportunity to access information in ways that suit their preferred way of thinking and prominent learning style;

- provide 'gateways' to develop numeracy, literacy and scientific skills and competencies through other intelligences;

- commit ourselves to raise our own awareness in order for us to see all children as intelligent;

- provide a broad and stimulating curriculum and an environment in which children feel secure enough to take risks with their learning;

- enhance our curriculum planning to provide challenging activities which cater for multiple intelligences and a range of abilities;

- create for all individuals a creative, positive and supportive learning environment in which children's self-esteem and emotional intelligence blossom;

- gain an appreciation of how the brain works, how we learn and the conditions for optimum learning, including the importance of diet, good health, exercise and emotional states;

- use recognition, affirmation and praise (RAP) to motivate and encourage optimum learning and achievement;

- teach listening skills, thinking skills, give time for thinking and methods to promote memory, retention and recall, including: the importance of review, mind mapping (see pages 88 and 89), Brain Gym® and novel ways of recording;

- develop effective target-setting for each individual;

- teach children about multiple intelligences, and raise their awareness of their own preferred learning styles and the conditions for optimum learning;

- provide opportunities for children to demonstrate their learning and to be, at times, teachers of others;

- use a range of teaching methods including accelerated learning techniques;

- be models of good learners and demonstrate a fascination for learning;

- clarify current practice and determine future approaches to teaching and learning;

- convey our philosophy about teaching and learning;

- provide an agreed framework which underpins all areas of the curriculum;

- reduce within-school variation by building consistency of high-quality teaching based on what is known about learning;

- raise levels of attainment for all pupils, enabling them to achieve their personal best;

- develop confident, disciplined and enquiring learners who are able to make informed choices;

- foster self-esteem, and increase each individual's learning power, by developing the seven Rs of effective learners: readiness, responsibility, resourcefulness, resilience, remembering, reflectiveness and reciprocity.

Definition of learning

Learning is difficult to define. Most definitions *refer* to learning; however, they tend to highlight teaching styles rather than learning styles.

This policy is based on research

From our research into teaching and learning we have come to some agreement on the following:

Learning is a personal process

Learning is not something that can be done to you, but is something you go through with the support and aid of others. So learning is a social activity.

Learning takes place at a level beyond what you already know

If learners already know something, understanding may be reinforced but it will not be new learning. Learning takes place just beyond what we already understand.

There are optimal conditions for learning

This is when the learner enters a state of 'flow' (as coined by Mihaly Csikszentmihalyi), which occurs when the current level of skill or understanding of the learner is closely matched with the appropriate degree of challenge; when learning goals are clear, relevant feedback is given at the point of learning, and the learner is able to devote attention to the task in hand because the learning environment reduces anxiety and is conducive to creating, within the learner, a state of *relaxed alertness*. This is affected by an individual's motivation, which in turn is affected by a range of influences, including self-esteem, stress and purpose.

Learning is affected by physical factors

This includes the individual's health, diet, hydration and feelings of well-being. The physical nature of the learning environment also has a powerful influence on learning.

Learning involves receiving and processing new information

For each individual learner this takes place in different ways.

Learning is a consequence of thinking

Learning is always a consequence of thinking ... As we think *about* and *with* the content that we are learning, we truly learn it.

Learning is learnable

Learning involves the development of skills that will support further learning. These skills include co-operation, collaboration, communication, the ability to question, reflect and reason, and the ability to think in a range of ways. This involves the development of 'learning power' – the various 'R's mentioned earlier in this policy.

Learning is messy

Learning is not a linear process. The learner constructs new learning onto what is already known. The process matches the way the brain, literally, makes connections.

Our Teaching for Learning Policy recognizes research findings into the way the human brain works. These include:

- Good health is important to an effective brain.

- Learning is optimized in a supportive, learning environment in which 'relaxed alertness' is promoted.

- Learning is about making connections.

- Learners need to see the big picture.

- Children need to know the intended learning outcomes.

- Work needs to address children's different learning styles.

- Each person has a portfolio of intelligences.

- Time needs to be created for complex thinking to take place.

- To embed learning, learners need to demonstrate learning.

- Review for recall and retention is a vital part of learning.

As previously stated, recognition is given to each of the above research findings. The implications from these for teaching and learning at St Vincent's Catholic Primary School are outlined below:

1. Good health is important to an effective brain

- Lack of sleep makes the brain inefficient.

- Diet and exercise play a big part in enabling the brain to work effectively.

- Regular intakes of water stop the brain from becoming dehydrated.

- High levels of oxygen are important to brain functioning.

- The right foods provide the brain with the nutrients it needs.

Policy Statements

- We provide frequent and easy access to water.

- We teach the children about healthy living.

- We provide an ethos which optimizes learning – low stress/ appropriate challenge.

- We encourage children to eat healthy snacks.

- We communicate to parents about research into learning.

In Practice

- The children have access to water fountains and are encouraged to use them.

- Newsletters contain information about learning and how the brain works.

- Children are encouraged to bring a suitable water bottle into school and to drink regularly.

- Health education is part of the curriculum.

- We are working towards the Healthy Schools' Award.

- PE lessons always include something about the effect and importance of exercise.

- The school kitchen provides a healthy menu and advice is offered to parents who provide their children with a packed lunch.

2. Learning is optimized in a supportive, learning environment

- Relaxed alertness, not stress, is the best state for learning.

- Learners who are stressed cannot learn.

- 'Relaxed alertness' involves a combination of being aware of what is going on, being ready to act and move forward, and being sufficiently relaxed so as not to be inhibited by stress.

- Our emotional system drives our 'attentional' system, which drives learning and memory.

Policy Statements

- We work to develop children's self-esteem.

- We promote learning through positive encouragement.

- We provide an ethos which optimizes learning – low stress/high challenge.

- We teach children about emotional intelligence.

In Practice

- Teachers are quick to praise and slow to criticize.

- Teachers emphasize the importance of learning.

- Teachers develop a high expectation culture.

- Positive behaviour is recognized, affirmed and praised (RAP).

- Teachers model enthusiasm for learning and emotional intelligence.

- Each classroom is free from intimidation – a 'no put-down zone'.

- When criticism is necessary it is constructive and directed at the behaviour or performance rather than at the child as a person.

- Children are encouraged to take risks with their learning.

- Standard operating procedures provide familiar frameworks and minimize things that interfere with learning.

- Children are kept informed of any changes.

- We create and celebrate a sense of collective achievement.

- Humour is used a lot to diffuse situations.

- Sarcasm is never used.

- Children are taught that failure is a vital part of learning.

- Children are made to feel that they 'belong'.

- Each class has a weekly circle-time session. This is an occasion when children 'check-in' and are 'recognized' and 'affirmed' by each other.

- The adults within the school create a supportive learning environment.

- Children work in supportive, co-operative teams.

- Teachers plan learning activities and scaffold learning in ways that balance the current level of skill with the appropriate level of challenge and support.

- Positive role models are used and affirmation posters are on display.

3. Learning is about making connections

- The brain literally makes connections inside our heads.

- Learning takes place when the brain makes connections between new experiences and older experiences.

- The more connections that are made the 'deeper' the learning.

Policy Statements

- We show children the connections between what they are learning now with what they have already learned.

- We use prediction exercises to access what is already known and to pre-process thinking about the content to come.

- Whenever possible, we relate what we teach to the children's own experiences.

- We provide the learners with the learning outcomes, the keywords and the questions they will be able to answer by the completion of the experiences.

In Practice

- Lessons start with an introduction in which teachers remind children what has gone before – review/preview.

- Teachers help to consolidate existing connections.

- Learning outcomes are made explicit, displayed in child-friendly language and children are encouraged to articulate and share them in order to gain clearer understanding.

- Learning objectives are turned into 'key questions' because the brain continues to find answers.

- Lessons are frequently related to the local environment, which is used as a major teaching resource.

4. Children need to see the big picture

- Learning works best when children can be helped to link all the different aspects of their work.

- Children learn better when they can see things in context and see the point of what they are doing.

- We can often assume that the pupils know the point of what we are asking them to do.

Policy Statements

- We start each unit of work with an overview of what children will be doing and learning.

- We begin each lesson by making the learning objective explicit and show how their work fits into the big picture.

- We make the links with content and process explicit by explaining what we do and why we do it; encourage meta-cognition and learner self-knowledge.

- We continue pre-processing the questions learners will have begun to ask themselves.

- We end each lesson by reviewing the intended learning objective and giving children the opportunity to check their own understanding.

In Practice

- Every time a class starts a new topic or unit of work, the teacher spends time talking with the children about what it involves, what they already know about it, what they will be learning and what they will be doing. Children are also given the opportunity to find answers to questions they set for themselves.

- Teachers develop a culture of high expectation.

- In lessons, teachers find ways of showing children the practical implications of what they are learning – the learning will help ensure future success – WIFM (what's in it for me?).

- Teachers impress on the children the importance of developing learning skills and that learning is a lifelong activity.

- Links with everyday life are made.

- Teachers continue to alleviate anxiety by creating clarity and reminding the children about support strategies.

- Teachers begin to challenge understanding.

- Teachers engage curiosity.

- There is a review session at the beginning of each lesson when the teacher reminds children about what the unit of work is about and how the lesson relates to it.

- The learning objectives are reviewed regularly within the lesson.

- Key vocabulary is identified.

- The children are encouraged to reflect on their own learning and on their current level of understanding.

- There is a plenary session at the end of each lesson, which provides an opportunity for reviewing the learning objective, for children to demonstrate their learning and for the teacher to remind the children how it fits into the unit of work as a whole. The teacher also tells the children what they will be doing next in order to give them the opportunity to find out information about it and give them thinking time.

5. Learners need to know the intended learning outcomes

- Learners need to know what they are supposed to be learning.

- It is difficult to reach a learning target if you do not know what the target is.

- Learners tend to learn more effectively those things which they want to learn.

- All learners are starting from different points.

- The brain continues to work on questions to find answers.

Policy Statements

- We tell the students what they will have achieved by the end of the lesson.

- We provide opportunities for pupils to discuss the targets.

- We provide formal and informal opportunities for pupils to set personal learning targets.

- We differentiate the learning.

In Practice

- Learning targets are made explicit and visually reinforced.

- National Curriculum learning objectives are translated into 'child-friendly' language.

- Time is devoted to ensure the pupils understand the learning objectives and the tasks that will be carried out to achieve them.

- Learning objectives are turned into 'key questions'.

- Planning templates are sometimes used to develop structured outcomes.

- The learning is chunked into bite-sized pieces.

- Differentiated learning targets are set. These are described as MUST, COULD and SHOULD.

6. Work needs to address different learning styles

- There are three main learning styles: *visual*, *auditory* and *kinesthetic*.

- Most children are able to use all three styles.

- About one-fifth of all children have a very strong preference for one style only.

Policy Statements

- We try to identify the preferred learning styles of all children.

- Whenever possible, we provide a balance of visual, auditory and kinesthetic inputs in each lesson.

- Where appropriate, we adapt learning activities to suit the preferred learning styles of particular children.

In Practice

- Many lessons include activities involving different learning styles.

- All topics and units of work include a range of activities that cater for different learning styles.

- Teachers, when appropriate, provide activities that suit the children's own particular learning styles.

7. Each child has a portfolio of intelligences

- Intelligence is not just one factor.

- Each child has multiple intelligences, which are different but equal in status.

- Children can be intelligent in some areas but less intelligent in others.

- Children can sometimes access work that they would otherwise find difficult by using their stronger intelligences.

- Successful learning follows most quickly when new learning is 'fixed' in as many forms of intelligence as possible.

Policy Statements

- We view each child as intelligent and identify areas of strength.

- We provide activities appropriate to a range of intelligences to enable access to and the development of other intelligences.

- We provide a broad curriculum so that all children will be enabled to develop their strengths.

- The Foundation Stage Profile is used to influence planning for the various areas of learning.

In Practice

- The school finds ways of giving appropriate weight to all curriculum subjects, not allowing any to be 'squeezed out'.

- Teachers treat all children in a positive way – recognizing, affirming and praising good effort, work and behaviour.

- Teachers know children's strengths and build on them, often using them as a way into areas of relative weakness (for example, using a child's strength in art as a starting point for maths or writing).

- Curriculum provision includes 'rich tasks' that bring the curriculum to life by making the activities relevant. These tasks are cross-curricular which promote coherence and reduce fragmentation.

8. Time needs to be created for complex thinking to take place

- Children need time for reflective thinking.

- The mind can solve complex issues only by sifting and sorting the information it has been given over a period of time.

Policy Statements

- We provide children with thinking time.

- We teach a range of thinking skills.

- We incorporate quality time for review and reflection in every lesson.

In Practice

- Teachers give children advance notice of tasks that are going to require thoughtful preparation.

- Children are encouraged to utilize a range of thinking skills.

- Many lessons have brief review breaks when children are asked to think – and perhaps make notes – about what they have been doing.

- Children are encouraged to reflect on their own thinking and learning.

9. To embed learning, learners need to demonstrate learning

- To demonstrate something is to truly know it.
- We tend to remember 90 per cent of what we teach.
- Knowing that we are going to have to teach something focuses attention.
- As we teach, we learn.
- When someone can perform their learning it shows understanding.
- Demonstration of learning is a critical part of formative assessment.

Policy Statements

- We think of ways children can demonstrate or perform their learning.
- Demonstration of learning is linked to planning.
- We teach children strategies that help demonstrate their learning.
- We learn in a social context.
- We teach children how to use ICT to support their learning.

In Practice

- We provide feedback at the point of learning.
- We encourage children to articulate what they are learning (pole-bridging).
- We teach children 'mind mapping' to support presentations.
- We teach children co-operative learning strategies, for example pair-share, Rally Robin, each one–teach one, and so on.
- Children produce learning posters for other children.
- Children use PowerPoint.
- Children devise tests for one another.
- Children demonstrate their understanding.

10. Review is a vital part of learning

- Review is vital for embedding learning into the long-term memory.
- Learning without review is like filling the bath without the plug in.
- Since the brain cannot pay attention to everything, uninteresting, boring or emotionally flat lessons simply will not be remembered.
- Effective learners review their learning.

Policy Statements

- We provide quality time for review.

- Learning objectives are reviewed several times in a lesson.

- We build novelty into lessons.

- We teach thinking skills to support review.

- We teach memory techniques.

In Practice

- Lessons start and end with a preview/review.

- Children are taught 'blue hat thinking' to aid reflection.

- Brain breaks provide an opportunity to review learning objectives and reflection points.

- Team planning helps to produce interesting and creative activities that are memorable.

- Review happens at the end of a lesson, end of the day, end of the week, a month later, and so on.

- Display is used to support learning and develop memory.

- Memory techniques are taught.

- Pupils receive regular and frequent feedback with clear strategies for improvement.

Chapter 12

Case Study

Personalizing schools

Max Coates

Enumclaw High School, Washington, DC

Introduction

Most education systems are founded on a belief that there is a body of knowledge that must be understood in order for the individual to participate in and contribute to the society in which they live. In the main this is still significantly content based. The current debate about personalization and personalized learning has not significantly changed this focus. Consider the following taken from *A National Conversation about Personalised Learning*:

> For teachers, it means a focus on their repertoire of teaching skills, their subject specialisms and their management of the learning experience. Personalized learning requires a range of whole class, group and individual teaching, learning and ICT strategies to transmit knowledge, to instil key learning skills and to accommodate different paces of learning. (DfES, 2004b)

In the above extract there are some fascinating creedal statements. It is set under a sub-heading of 'Effective teaching and learning strategies'. In a document that concentrates on learning there is an almost unconscious slip into the primacy of teaching: learning 'requires a range of whole class, group and individual teaching'. There is an emphasis on the transmission of knowledge: are students included in a neurological wireless network? The terminology 'instil key learning skills' presents a deeply hierarchical view of education which suggests the expert practitioner will implant these like a cognitive pacemaker. Of course, there appears to be a reference to an agreed learning skill-set for which there is by no means a consensus. Intriguingly, there is the statement about accommodation of 'different paces of learning' if only learning was that easy. Differentiation cannot be understood in terms of time; mathematical or literacy development cannot be brought onto a level playing field by allocating more curriculum time.

The Qualifications and Curriculum Authority (QCA) provides a further interesting dimension to the personalization debate. In its document, *Designing a Personalised Curriculum for Alternative Provision at Key Stage 4*, the client group for personalized learning is identified as:

> In 2003, up to 75,000 young people across England participated in education outside mainstream secondary schools, in LEA-managed or brokered alternative provision. This provision includes that provided by pupil retrieval units (PRUs),

hospital teaching services, home tuition services and virtual (or e-) learning centres; and provision commissioned by the LEA from FE colleges, training providers, employers, voluntary sector organizations, community services, youth services, youth offending teams and other local agencies. In addition, many schools directly commission placements from similar agencies for students remaining on their roll.

Students accessing this provision at Key Stage 4 include:

- *those who have been excluded permanently from school*

- *those presenting challenging behaviour and at risk of exclusion*

- *those whose attendance at Key Stage 3 has been exceptionally low*

- *those who are sick, in hospital or with medical needs, including those with psychiatric needs*

- *young carers*

- *pregnant schoolgirls and young mothers*

- *highly mobile students (for example travellers, refugees, asylum seekers, young people whose families are in crisis)*

- *those in and out of custody*

- *school refusers and phobics.*

Inclusive education aims to respond to and anticipate diverse learner characteristics. Most of these students are possibly unable to access the mainstream curriculum because of the gap between what they need and what is available at the time, not because of any deficiency in themselves. (QCA, 2004b: page 4)

A nearby comprehensive school offers the following understanding of personalizing education. In its recent parents' newsletter there was an assurance that the school was at the forefront of the personalizing learning agenda. This was supported by citing programmes for the gifted and talented and the support for students with special educational needs. This was seen as a definitive statement.

The Specialist Schools' Trust has recently commissioned Professor David Hargreaves, the former chief executive of the Qualifications and Curriculum Authority, to produce its pamphlet on personalized learning. His proposal is that there should be nine 'gateways' which largely correspond to the view outlined by the Department for Education and Skills but include 'student voice' and 'new technologies'. Hargreaves suggests the use of the word 'personalizing' rather than personalized because it would identify an on-going process rather than a decision. Like the government, he stresses the economic mantra that personalized learning should not be equated with one to one tuition for all pupils. (Shaw and Paton, 2004)

The perception of personalizing learning remains confused and confusing. It ranges from a significant transformational dream to tweaking the teaching process to provision for the gifted and talented, those with learning difficulties and those who are excluded for other reasons. Perhaps it is pertinent to ask more fundamental questions: 'How can education in the twenty-first century support the development of twenty-first century learners and what would such schools look like?' If 90 per cent of what we know will be out of date in six years time, does this mean that the secondary school is equipping its students up to the age of 24. Alvin Toffler, in *Future Shock* (1970), was one of the first to highlight the impact and consequences of the knowledge explosion. He concludes that:

 The illiterate of the 21st century will not be those who cannot read and write but those who cannot learn and unlearn.

(page 323)

A moment's reflection on how we learn as an individual is likely to suggest a very different context to that experienced in many schools. This has been brought into greater focus by the University of Bristol's Effective Lifelong Learning Inventory (ELLI). This work was undertaken by Broadfoot, Claxton and Deakin Crick (2005); it identified seven key dimensions that supported an individual's motivation or power to learn. These included developing resilience as a learner, the ability to make meaning, critical curiosity, creativity and learning relationships. The research concludes that over time, and particularly through the course of formal learning, children currently become weaker as learners. At the same time they become more dependent on teachers and others to help them learn and less able to cope with mistakes and failure.

This research points to the need for the individual to feel personal significance and in control of their situation for appropriate learning to take place. The school must support the emotional needs of the individual; it must be a place that provides lowered levels of stress but supports challenging activities. The school should also support the development of a community of learning. Through the creative use of space there must be a move from a social gathering ground to a building that focuses the groups and sub-groups on learning together. The experience of a child feeling like a corpuscle in a chaotic arterial system will not support learning.

The following are not held to be definitive but are twelve principles for the design of school buildings derived from the work of Dr Jeffery Lackney (2001):

1. Rich, stimulating environments – colour, texture, 'teaching architecture', displays created by students (not teachers) so that students have connection and ownership of the product.

2. Places for group learning – breakout spaces, alcoves, table groupings to facilitate social learning and stimulate the social brain; turning breakout spaces into living rooms in which conversations take place.

3. Linking indoor and outdoor places – movement, engaging the motor cortex, linked to the cerebral cortex, for oxygenation.

4. Corridors and public places containing symbols of the school community's larger purpose, to provide coherency and meaning that increases motivation.

5. Safe places – reduce threat, especially in urban settings.

6. Variety of places – provide a variety of places of different shapes, colour, light, nooks and crannies.

7. Changing displays – changing the environment: interacting with the environment stimulates brain development. Provide display areas that allow for stage-set type constructions to further push the envelope with regard to environmental change.

8. Have all resources available – provide educational, physical and a variety of settings in close proximity to encourage rapid development of ideas generated in a learning episode. This is an argument for wet areas/science, computer-rich workspaces all integrated and not segregated. Multiple functions and cross-fertilization of ideas are the primary goals.

9. Flexibility – a common principle in the past continues to be relevant. Many dimensions of flexibility of place are reflected in other principles.

10. Active/passive places – students need places for reflection and retreat away from others for intrapersonal intelligence as well as places for active engagement for interpersonal intelligence.

11. Personalized space – the concept of homebase needs to be emphasized more than the metal locker or the desk. This speaks to the principle of uniqueness; the need to allow learners to express their self-identity; personalize their special places; and areas to express territorial behaviours.

12. The community-at-large as the optimal learning environment – the need to find ways to fully utilize all urban and natural environments as the primary learning setting. The school as the fortress of learning needs to be challenged, and conceptualized more as a resource-rich learning centre that supplements lifelong learning. Technology, distance learning, community and business partnerships, home-based learning, all need to be explored as alternative organizational structures for educational institutions of the present and future.

Lackney's argument is that diversity of design will support learning styles and not constrain education by supporting a transient trend.

As long as education has a primary focus on content rather than process and a curriculum that is highly subject specific, the building envelope and the structure of the school day will remain largely stagnant. A visit to the latest schools will reveal greater energy efficiency, décor, a better reception area, an improved ICT infrastructure but few other significant changes. An examination of schools where there has been a change to the school day, for example, the introduction of the continental day, will see timings largely driven by local expediency and childcare provision.

Thinking outside of the box

Since the 1988 Educational Reform Act, UK schools have been significantly centrally directed and target driven. Running schools in this climate has not always had the fun factor. Creativity and innovation have often been driven by marketing and not by educational objectives. As the head of a school in what was euphemistically called challenging circumstances, I asked my local education authority link adviser/inspector for advice. His first response was to advise a change in the colour of the school blazer. It is sometimes easier to focus on image rather than substance.

Can the personalizing learning agenda be taken forward? A number of schools, particularly in the US, have adopted radical approaches to this issue. One of the most striking is that of Enumclaw High School, Washington, DC. The following case study (Stanford University, 2003) is challenging and intriguing, of course it remains very much work in progress with few clear outcomes at this stage.

Enumclaw High School is a suburban–rural high school serving approximately 1,600 students east of Tacoma, Washington, DC. It is the sole high school in a unified district with a population that is 93 per cent white in addition to small percentages of Latino, native American, Asian and African-American students. Enumclaw was already a successful high school by traditional measures, but the staff and community became convinced that they could do better.

The Foundation Project director at Enumclaw High School, Jill Burns, came from a 'data driven district' where data were used as the lever to implement district policies. The approach taken at Enumclaw has been very different, and yet data have played a critical role in its reform process. A wider spread of data was also examined which was felt to provide a more objective perspective. 'State wide' data were examined, not just about schools but about jobs and the economy their students would be entering. This 'external data' served as the basis of discussions about what the school could change so that its students would be better prepared for both college and the world of work. At this point one of their eight research teams, the accountability team, which comprised eight teachers, chose to review 'internal data'. When this team of teachers presented its findings to the staff it had, so the director, believes:

> ... a much greater impact than if the data had been presented by administrators. The staff did not feel threatened by this approach, which built a picture of the need for change over time until a critical mass of staff agreement on the need for change had been reached. (Burns, 2001: page 1)

In addition to data on graduation rates, attendance, test scores, course pass–fail rates and discipline, the accountability team conducted surveys of parents and students to learn about their experiences with the school. These qualitative data sets, when collected and presented, 'almost had a more powerful impact than the quantitative data'. A notable reason for Enumclaw's success in using data to motivate the staff, and for the community to consider change, stems from the fact the data collected were not used to focus on how 'bad' the school was, or to suggest that teachers were not doing their jobs. Burns recalls:

> From the data we found that we were good, but that we could do even better; here was an opportunity to do something really amazing! (Burns, 2001: page 2)

Structures that support improved student learning

After several months of planning, Enumclaw High School had decided, by mid-2002, to redesign itself into seven small schools. Two 'partner schools' opened in autumn 2002 and five 'interest-based schools' opened in autumn 2003.

Staff voted early in the process to guarantee that no one would lose his or her job because of the redesign. Consequently, class sizes have not, and will not, change substantially in the smaller learning communities, remaining at a ratio (low in comparison to many nearby districts) of 26–1. Greater personalization will occur, however, through students staying with the same teacher for two to four years, with advisory and advocacy teams (the advisory team is a staff member and group of students meeting on a regular basis; the advocacy team will consist of a student, a parent or guardian, an adviser from the small school staff and a community member meeting three or four times a year), individualized learning plans and student choice of schools.

Learning about promising redesign efforts

While it is too early to discuss results in terms of students' grades and/or long-term academic performance measures, there is much about the process and the redesign plan adopted by Enumclaw that may inform other schools or districts considering conversions to smaller learning communities.

After Enumclaw School District received a School Grant from the Bill and Melinda Gates' Education Foundation in the spring of 2000, the small questions they thought they were asking rapidly became much larger ones. The school began a comprehensive reinvention process, spanning 18 months and including over 200 planning, training and research meetings. This led to the eventual redesign.

All of the schools in the community are developed around four shared values:

- High academic expectations. The call for high academic expectations for all students comes from the recognition that the economy has undergone major changes; low-skill jobs requiring minimal education are viewed as a thing of the past. Accordingly, all students in these small schools will be 'positioned to choose from all available post-high school options, including entrance into a four-year university'.

- Personalized student learning. A central part of Enumclaw's reinvention plan is to 'more deeply personalize the teaching and learning that occurs at our school'. They hope to find the spark that ignites each student's passion for learning by giving 'students and families choices of rich, unique learning environments that increase their understanding of the connections between school and the real world'. All seven of the schools will provide their students with personalized learning plans to meet their academic needs and goals, and connect them with an adult staff member who knows them well and can work to support them throughout their time at Enumclaw.

- Continuous staff development. Staff development has occurred throughout the reinvention process, with teachers playing a primary role in the eight staff research teams' committees that researched and designed the new schools, while focusing on the areas of 'literacy, instruction, small schools' structure, technology, staff development, student transition planning, quality organizational systems and performance accountability'. Beginning in the autumn of 2002, time was put into the schedule on a weekly basis for teachers and support staff 'to learn, improve their teaching skills, plan together, develop their small schools' curricula, and to discuss the needs of their students'.

- Performance accountability. Before the reinvention of Enumclaw took place, the whole staff agreed on school-wide standards of learning that all the small schools would have to adhere to in order to guarantee equal learning opportunities for all students on the campus. In addition, surveys of the community followed by candid discussions asked, 'what do you value in terms of student results/abilities beyond test scores; what evidence of student progress beyond test scores would you like to have?' In partial response to these meetings, teachers are creating a school report card that will reflect student learning beyond just letter grades.

Partner schools

The two partner schools currently reflect the greatest departure from the former Enumclaw High in terms of scheduling and instructional approach. While still occupying space on the same campus, they operate largely as 'self-contained independent schools'.

Both of the partner schools began with a capacity enrolment of 150 9–12th grade students after a lottery process was used due to the high number of applicants. Each school has a staff of six teachers and a special education specialist. Students will have the same teachers for all four years, creating a personalized environment where teachers and students know each other well. All students will develop their own personalized learning plan, with input from parents/guardians and their adviser.

One of these, the Adventure School, plans to add a community member to each student's advocacy team, which will meet three or four times throughout the year.

A specific review of one of the partner schools: Enumclaw Adventure School

Enumclaw Adventure School is the most autonomous and, as the name suggests, the most adventurous of the new schools. Generally, students do not take classes outside of this smaller learning community, although individual exceptions are sometimes made. Learning in Enumclaw Adventure School is highly integrated and very hands-on. The staff wants students to 'discover the connections between different subject areas through theme-based curriculum, internships, community service and other self-directed educational adventures'. Students work in both subject-based and interdisciplinary classrooms on campus for several weeks and then spend one to two weeks off-site applying and advancing their learning in real-world contexts. When students return to campus they plan and present exhibitions of what they have learned. All students in the Adventure School must take the SAT (preparation seminars are offered to all students), and all students are expected to apply to enter a post-secondary educational institution, be it a four-year college, junior college or technical school.

Interest-based schools

The five interest-based schools have larger populations (from 200–300 students) and larger faculties (12–14) than the partner schools. These schools' personalities initially will come more from their thematic orientations than from their instructional approaches, although, like the partner schools, they have an emphasis on 'internships' and community service in order to 'ignite our students' passion for learning' and 'allow them to see a connection between their learning and the world in which they live'. Each of these five schools will provide all students with a 'rigorous core academic programme for 9th and 10th grade, a flexible individualized advanced preparation programme for 11th and 12th grade, course learning standards, an advisory programme and an individual learning plan and transition plan for every student'. All five will offer all students the courses they would need to enter a four-year college, if they so choose. Special efforts will be made to interest students in colleges through university and community college partnerships.

Autonomy

Both partner schools have designed their curriculum so that their students can continue to participate in campus-wide sports and extra-curricular activities. They have a lunch hour that overlaps with students in the other schools. They have flexible schedules that allow for extensive inter-disciplinary teaching, students working at their own pace, and considerable time spent doing hands-on learning while off-site.

All of the interest-based schools within the Enumclaw facility operate on the same time schedule, at least during the first two years of the plan's implementation, so students can 'cross over' between schools for classes they may want or need. Aware that research indicates that students benefit most from truly autonomous small schools, Enumclaw plans to determine two years from now 'whether the logistics will allow us to move toward more separate and distinctive small schools'. In another form of 'cross over', a partnership with the local community college allows Enumclaw to offer an 'early college institute', through which students in any of the small schools can receive an associate's degree by the time they leave high school and take advanced placement classes. A special effort is being made to recruit a cohort that might not typically consider going to college.

The current plan is to have some flexibility in terms of changing from one school to another. Students will select a small school in the spring of their 8th grade year and again in the spring of their 10th grade year so that changes in student interest can be accommodated. In response to one of the '23 frequently asked questions' answered on the school's website, families are assured: 'We do not want to create small schools that force our children to make career decisions during their developmental middle school and high school years.'

Enumclaw's strategy was very much to redesign itself in ways that are best for the students and at a pace that would be supported by their faculty and community. Jill Burns (2001) recognizes that:

> *The community just wouldn't have allowed it without some compromise and a phase-in process that allowed, at least at first, for things like crossover. We are very much proceeding with the feeling that experience will build belief. The faculty, too, needs to develop the confidence that they can take care of all the kids' needs as a group rather than continuing to rely on the piecemeal approach.*
> (page 3)

There are already signs of this growing confidence. Several of the teams are starting to see advantages to not being tied to a central time schedule and are wondering about the possibilities that would come with greater autonomy. Conversions at already moderately successful schools may prove to be more organic or evolutionary, so long as shortcomings result in continued movement forward rather than retreats into the old structure.

Although some may adjust their names and foci in due course, the five schools in the original plan are described as follows:

- The School of Design and Production: this school will facilitate learning for students interested in the visual arts, designing and manufacturing products that improve the world we live in.

- The School of Global Studies and Business: this school facilitates learning for students interested in our increasingly interconnected world and how business influences personal, national and world growth.

- The School of Innovation and Technology: this school facilitates learning for students interested in science and technology and how new developments will change our world.

- The School of Culture and Performing Arts: this school will facilitate learning for students interested in the interaction of self-expression and its impact on people's lives.

- The School of Discovery and Human Resources: this school will facilitate learning for students interested in improving quality of life through scientific investigation and connections to community, human and natural resources.

Rethinking budgets and staffing

As mentioned earlier, the Enumclaw High School staff decided very early in the process that no one would lose his or her job as a result of the restructuring. Teachers who had done a lot of reading about school change argued that everything could and should be on the table for discussion, including budget and jobs. Conversely, there was a feeling that staff ownership and support required job security. This did not mean that everyone was going to be guaranteed the same job they have now:

 A counselor may not still have A-L, a classified staff member's job description might change, as might a teacher's assignment.

(Burns, 2001: page 5)

Some of the classified staff were assigned to specific schools, while others continued to hold central, campus-wide jobs. Three administrators divide up primary responsibility for the different schools while continuing to work as a team responsible for the whole campus. There may be some changes in staffing due to natural wastage: retirement, relocation and so on.

In Enumclaw's partner schools, every teacher applied for and received a state waiver allowing them to teach outside of their subject area, but every teacher has expertise in the area in which they are teaching. For example, one teacher had previously taught English in a private school, although she was not accredited in that subject. Information distributed to the community made the expertise of all the teachers clear and concise. Teachers in the interest-based schools are not as familiar with interdisciplinary teaching, so most will continue to teach in their specific subject area, at least in the initial phase. Experience and professional development are expected to lead to more innovative instruction and the need for additional out-of-subject waivers.

Managing curricular and extra-curricular trade-offs

The extensive choice of classes in the old comprehensive structure will be countered by increased personalization and curricular focus in different ways and to different degrees in each of the new Enumclaw schools. The Adventure School prefers to allow very little 'crossover' for other electives. Students in this school are generally expected to take Spanish as their foreign language and their ethnic homogeneity does not create the de-facto segregation resulting from the same practice at some more diverse schools. Spanish, French and German will be offered in the other schools, and students will be allowed to crossover to take a language not offered in their school.

The Performing Arts School is redefining electives through a more integrated curriculum. Electives, such as band, chorus, drama, and so on, are offered within the school day and crossover will be allowed for students who wish to participate. It is expected that small schools will have to make some compromises in order to allow students to do this. The timetable has not yet been fully developed and some teams of teachers are beginning to ask about the possibility of greater autonomy. Athletics is offered to all students after school and is therefore open to students from any of Enumclaw's seven schools.

A few teachers in the Adventure School have taught advanced placement and hope to coach students who wish to take an advanced placement exam. The other schools will take advantage of a partnership with the local community college, which allows Enumclaw to offer an early college institute. Through this programme, students in any of the small schools can receive an AP (advanced placement) by the time they leave high school. In addition to students ordinarily drawn to this kind of programme, the institute makes a special effort to attract students who will be among the first in their family to attend college. There is still discussion as to when and how the timetable should be built in order to allow students to take classes in both a small school and the institute. Some wonder if the most driven parents are expecting that their children will be taking four or five classes in the institute. These students would still have an advisory at Enumclaw. One of the most important conversations going on now at Enumclaw is about 'rigour and student engagement', and it is the school's belief that, by gaining a better understanding of these two issues through quality professional development, all students can be given the opportunity to do high-level intellectual work.

Ensuring equity and choice in student and teacher grouping

Teacher teams

Openness was an important theme in much of the redesign process at Enumclaw, and this was especially true in decisions around staffing. In the case of the two partner schools that opened first, two groups of teachers realized that they were interested in taking the reforms further than the rest of the staff. The whole staff was asked if they would allow these teachers to design two more distinctive and innovative schools, and they were given the staff's blessing to go their own way. These two self-selected teams of teachers held open planning meetings and, in the process, filled out their staff with other teachers who attended these meetings and became excited by what they heard.

In the case of the interest-based schools, a committee was put in charge of creating a staff assignment process, which the whole staff was asked to approve. A form was created on which staff indicated the school in which they wanted to work or the other staff members with whom they wanted to be teamed. They were also asked to indicate which of these two was most important to them.

Perhaps due to unfamiliarity with the autonomy arising from the new structure, the staff came to the conclusion that this was an 'administrative decision' and turned it over to the committee to make their best judgement. Jill Burns, the Gates' Foundation Project director, acting as a full-time consultant for Enumclaw throughout the process, explains:

> ... the administration wasn't comfortable with solely owning that process because, up to that point, everything had been shared work and lots of people had been involved.

So, the administration invited the staff to join a team that would make these decisions. One of the members of this new team was the union representative; another was elected by the staff. In addition, all meeting times of this group were posted and anyone wishing to come and 'listen to the conversation' was welcome. Going into the selection process everyone knew that each school would have a special education teacher in order to properly meet the legal requirements and educational needs of those students.

As a result of this very open process everyone was able to receive their first choice of assignment, with the exception of two teachers. While an appeal process had been set up, ultimately, it was not needed. In fact, later, when staff movement created the opportunity for one of the two to get their first choice, she had already bonded with her team and chose not to move. Those involved frequently emphasized that the committed and satisfied teams and the comfortable work environment found at Enumclaw High School are a result of the way no part of this process was conducted behind closed doors.

Classified staff was, in some cases, assigned to specific schools and in some cases kept central jobs serving the whole campus. Job descriptions changed, but no jobs were lost.

Students

All students at Enumclaw were given the opportunity to apply to the two new partner schools. When it was found that applicants exceeded the number of spaces available, a lottery system was created. Clearly, interest in the new schools was high; in fact, friction developed in the community when late applications were accepted and treated equally in the lottery with applications that had met the deadline. The schools tried to maintain a gender balance, with no greater than a 20 per cent difference at each grade level. An attempt was made to make sure that the sizes of the 9th, 10th, 11th and 12th grades were relatively balanced as well. Otherwise, it was a blind lottery system with no consideration given to any other factor.

Implementing the redesign

Enumclaw opened its two partner schools in the autumn of 2002 and opened the remaining five interest-based schools in the autumn of 2003. The partner schools were opened first due to a high level of enthusiasm generated by their respective staff's more extensive research on smaller learning communities. School leaders also realized that the most enthusiastic innovators could provide insight and examples for subsequent teacher-leaders as the partner schools' plans are put into practice. Jill Burns (2001) thinks that:

> ... experience will build belief and confidence among the staff to rely on themselves in more and more autonomous settings is on the rise. (page 6)

Enumclaw has used a very thorough change process, building capacity and desire for change among its staff and within their community one step at a time. Having a project director with considerable expertise and the ability to focus entirely on this effort undoubtedly was key in this regard. The decision to convert all four grades at once (rather than phase-in the new schools one grade at a time) was a bold one, but the consensus was 'if this is good for kids, we should just do it now'. On the other hand, the leadership team was very aware that pushing the staff or the community too far too fast would not result in successful change. So, while recognizing that research indicates autonomy is a key factor in a small school's success, Enumclaw has made compromises. There will be a phase-in period for the interest-based schools allowing 'crossover' to other schools for electives during the first two years. At that point Enumclaw will re-examine its crossover policy and consider whether or not to move towards greater autonomy. As teams begin to plan for next autumn, experience is again building belief and confidence – some school teams are beginning to ask about operating more on their own schedule in order to best reach their students.

Shared leadership within the school and public engagement

Enumclaw's story may best reveal how to conduct a thorough and effective change process. From the beginning the leadership team realized that it was not its task to provide the staff with a plan for change, but, as Jill Burns puts it, the team would be responsible for creating a process that would 'shift the thinking of the community from being compliant to being responsible for their own learning, their own change'. The leadership team was made up of two administrators, a teacher and Foundation Project director, Jill Burns, who was hired by the district and housed at the high school when the grant was received. Before they left for a two-week leadership conference at Harvard University, in the summer of 2000, they asked all members of staff to put in writing what they wanted to make sure was or was not a part of this process. From this list, the leadership team created guiding principles. Burns describes the two weeks spent off campus as a 'critical and transformative period', as they created an inclusive process that would involve a very democratic decision making and shared leadership. This was a significant shift for the principal, Terry Parker – a competent and well-liked leader, viewed by most as the man in charge. The staff initially did not believe he was changing his style of leadership, but, as the process unfolded and teachers' views shaped a new Enumclaw, there could be little doubt that this would be a collective effort.

In the autumn of 2000 the staff reviewed and revised the process and the initial set of guiding principles presented by the leadership team. They then engaged in a period of examining the question of 'Why change?'. An exciting renaissance of adult learning happened at Enumclaw. Teachers, who perhaps had not read about their craft since their certification programmes, created a culture of action-researchers there. They read about both education and organizational change. The staff and leadership team developed a deeper knowledge of the world they were preparing students to enter: the possibilities of new structures and how to move towards them. Burns (2001) describes the staff's reading of Roland S. Barthe's *Learning by Heart* (2001) as a 'pivotable point in preparation for the journey'. Their enthusiasm led them to not only invite Barthe as a speaker, but to design and wear T-shirts with his learning curve going off the chart on every pocket. 'I think he may have been a bit freaked out by that', says Burns with a smile, but his ideas on student learning, 'non-discussables' and adult behaviours all led to the creation of a 'team compact' expressing 'how we wanted to work together has stayed with us throughout the process'.

Another important aspect of the open and democratic process used by Enumclaw in its journey was the creation of research teams. In December of 2000 the staff and leadership team decided that there were eight key areas that needed to be researched:

- literacy

- instruction

- small school structure

- technology

- staff development

- student transition planning

- quality organizational systems

- performance accountability.

The study period was extensive, leading to a broad agreement that change was indeed crucial. Well over half of the staff volunteered to participate on one of the teams. Each research team chose a leader, who received training in meeting facilitation and working with adult learners. Each research team came up with standards and compared those standards to the 'current reality'. At the end of the year, those research teams submitted recommendations for the improvement of Enumclaw High School that were approved by the whole staff. Most committees met weekly and emailed the minutes from their meetings to staff the following day. In order to keep those faculty and staff members not on research teams involved, all staff development and staff meetings during this period were focused on the change process. Staff meetings were renamed 'staff learning seminars' and were no longer used merely for the distribution of information that could be communicated in other ways. By changing the focus and structure of regular staff meetings, the knowledge and experience base at Enumclaw broadened significantly.

In the summer of 2001 a leader from each research team took its team's recommendations to an in-house design institute while group teachers were sent to redesign institutes at Stanford University over the course of three weeks. This created an interesting dynamic. As each team returned to Enumclaw, they came back with new and different ideas about the structure that would best serve them. A new team would arrive at Stanford and want to change design aspects the previous week's team had created. Emails, phone calls and rumours flew up and down the West Coast! A revision team of students, staff and parents was established to work throughout the coming school year to 'synthesize, revise, and further develop these initial recommendations'. The revision team continued to hold and publicize its meetings every Tuesday afternoon for over a year. Since that time, a number of 'specialized ad-hoc committees' have been formed to investigate specific issues, such as scheduling and staffing. At the same time, a design team was established. It continues to serve as the high school reinvention steering committee and oversight board. The design team membership has included four students, eight parents and community members, and various staff members and school district administrators serving at different times throughout the past several years. Two groups of teachers returned from Stanford eager to move more quickly and more innovatively than the majority. The staff gave them permission to go their own way as long as they maintained school-wide learning standards and, as a result, the two partner schools opened in advance of the others schools. The design team's focus has primarily been on the five interest-based schools.

Public engagement began in the research stages, with surveys and focus groups that 'asked the community what they valued, what evidence beyond test scores would they like to see, what would they like students to be able to know and do when they graduate from Enumclaw High?' .By the time the school's staff was ready to begin presenting its plans, they were very skilled at communicating with the community. They had learned ways to involve the community and solicit opinions in the research process. The whole staff was very well informed and the community often commented that 'whoever we talk to about what is being done and why, we always get the same answers'. Parents were included on the design team as equal and active members. This last factor proved especially critical at one point when a group of parents that had so far not raised any questions, suddenly tried to organize against the plan. 'Having a group of parents who really felt ownership of the plan and were willing to fight for it did much more to address those parents' concerns than any response from the school staff had', explains Burns. A series of several 'community conversations' were held in the spring of 2002, in both the afternoons and the evenings, for 'interested community members to learn more about our reinvention programme, receive answers to questions, discuss reinvention issues and share feedback on the work done to date'. At many of their community meetings, Jamie Volmer's video, *Why Our Schools Need to Change*, was shown. A case for change was built first among the staff and then in the community, but the community played a role in the creation of the plan both through the open committee work and these public dialogues.

There was close liaison between Enumclaw High School and Stanford University. The latter have a specific interest in this type of redesign and can offer numerous case studies. Perhaps the most challenging aspect of the case study was the manner in which the school community embraced radical change but also started to ask questions that moved its thinking beyond the accepted.

Conclusion

It is apparent that achieving a consensus as to the nature of personalizing learning is still some way off. Education is still wedded to a content dominated, knowledge transmission model. The school building is a powerful icon of the prevailing pedagogical model. Clearly many schools have to work with buildings built under previous dispensations. However, the question must be raised about new buildings, which are, in the main, style changes rather than reflecting root and branch changes in the way learning takes place.

Enumclaw High School does not represent a model of schooling. It does, however, represent a challenging model for the management of innovative change. It is an engaging story as a school community asks deep questions and has the courage to make radical responses.

Consider the impact of the specialist school movement which has gained impetus over these last few years and looks likely to move towards 95 per cent of secondary schools in England having specialist status or being academies by 2008. We now have a plethora of technology, sports, music, expressive arts, business and enterprise colleges. Is there room for a specialist status for thinking skills or emotional literacy?

Chapter 13

Curriculum reform in Northern Ireland

Advisory Officer: Sharon Cousins

Southern Education and Library Board, Northern Ireland

 Learning's easy carried. Heaney (1991)

Introduction

There is something fascinating and unassailable about what is revealed by the perfect word or phrase; the perfect image making visceral connections. Heaney conveys in the above phrase the unconscious beliefs, values and assumptions of our culture in Northern Ireland. Hardly unique but powerful nevertheless, it asserts that we travel more easily in life's journey if we carry with us, in our hearts and heads, a precious learning or 'know-how': our passport to a successful future.

Educators around the globe are examining more carefully the imprint that curriculum and teaching leave on that learning journey. Crucial and fundamental questions are being posed: What knowledge do learners need in the twenty-first century? What does it mean to be a good learner? How can we nurture a love for learning that will endure in an uncertain and transient world? And with an increasingly sophisticated understanding of these epistemic processes, how can we reframe and redefine our education structures and curriculum to ensure that our response is apposite?

Northern Ireland is a small place, with a population about the size of Birmingham, UK. In this little corner of western Europe, with its unsettled, divisive past, the energy and commitment for change in many aspects of life is palpable.

Education in Northern Ireland is poised for a radical systemic change; there is commitment and potential to shape a brighter future for our children and young people who make up 27 per cent of the total population of 1.68 million. The proposed changes within our education system are emerging from a vision that many have held for some time; a revised curriculum is the cornerstone for its realization.

What was our starting point, and how did we determine the route to follow? What influences and drivers have made a change in direction and this journey possible, and what are the potential stumbling blocks?

This chapter explores the journey we have travelled, detailing:

- significant features of our current education system

- curriculum development

- the revised curriculum.

Significant features of the Northern Ireland education system

There are 1,288 schools in Northern Ireland: 99 nursery, 911 primary, 162 secondary, 70 grammar and 46 special schools. One-third of a million pupils are in statutory education and there are 20,335 teachers. The most distinctive characteristic of the educational system is 'segregation', mainly by religion, often by gender (44.3 per cent grammar and 19 per cent secondary are single sex), and, after the age of 11, by ability. Most pupils attend mainly Protestant or Catholic schools, with around 4.9 per cent of pupils attending integrated schools which have roughly equal numbers of Protestant and Catholic pupils. There is also a small number of Irish medium and other independent schools.

There is no difficulty with teacher supply: initial teacher education (ITE) providers are heavily oversubscribed and the standard of intake is very high with higher than average A-level points required for entry. Interestingly, but perhaps not surprisingly, the two University Colleges dedicated to ITE are segregated on the basis of religion.

A selective system of grammar and secondary schools has operated since 1947. At the age of 11, this selection process, in the form of transfer tests, takes place to separate out the more academically able, who attend the grammar schools.

Like Heaney's description of learning, the Irish proverb 'The woods would be very quiet if only the best birds sang' or, for those who may appreciate its cadence in Irish: '*Ba chiúin na coillte gan ach glór na n-éan is ceolmhaire*', is powerful and emotive. Its significance is apparent in our traditional selective system. We take pride in our academic excellence; grammar schools take centre stage in the achievement stakes. Vocational education is less highly regarded and pursued, for the most part, by those who have 'failed' the selection procedure at age 11. The talents of those who stumble at the first hurdle in the education race are ignominiously undervalued and self-worth has to be rebuilt in their journey through secondary school.

▶

In primary schools, time spent in preparing for the transfer tests narrows and distorts the Key Stage 2 curriculum. Achieving a high grade to gain entry to grammar school is the traditional academic route to a successful future; this is, for many, the learning that's 'easy carried'. 'Passing the test' has been a significant hurdle for 11 year olds for almost 60 years.

Research, commissioned by the Department of Education (DoE), into the effects of such a selective system has been ongoing since 1997 and findings are available in two major reports: *An Evaluation of the Craigavon Two-tier System* (Alexander et al., 1998) which focuses on the delayed selection system operating in the Craigavon area and providing an alternative to selection at age 11, and *The Effects of the Selective System of Secondary Education in Northern Ireland* (Gallagher and Smith, 2000) which examines the consequences of selection at age 11, finding that the system:

> ... *produces a disproportionate number of schools which combine low ability and social disadvantage in their enrolments, thereby compounding the educational disadvantages of both factors.* (page 46)

Measured in terms of examination results, this traditional system is successful. There is a real issue, however, as to how well this academic curriculum prepares young people for life and work in the twenty-first century.

Curriculum development

The lack of coherent purpose and direction in many primary and post-primary schools had been identified in the early 1980s. To resolve this, a process of review was initiated through staff and curriculum development projects: the Primary Guidelines and the 11–16 Programme. These were produced by the Northern Ireland Council for Education Development and were intended to help primary and post-primary schools to reflect and improve their approaches to learning and teaching, and to develop clear policies through whole-school collaborative enquiry. The guidelines, which were left to schools to interpret with little or no support, while valuable in many schools, were not moving quickly enough and perceived to be too ephemeral. That period of unhurried professional discourse is fondly referred to as the 'golden, halcyon era'. The imposed statutory curriculum, the sting in the tail of the 1980s, left such hedonistic reflection in limbo; the gentle undulating development of the curriculum landscape was perniciously blotted.

Few can forget the frenetic, mechanistic reforms emanating from the Education Reform Act in England in 1988: an edifice of control without systemic consensus. One year later, this monstrosity of legislation became the Education Reform Order in Northern Ireland. Here, too, the obsession with standards, focus on basics and a contentious assessment system fitted the wider accountability agenda and has pervaded schools and classrooms for over a decade, promulgated through a monolithic curriculum which was, as intended, essentially 'teacher-proof'. The hegemony of subjects and content in this reductionist model of curriculum characterized reform in the early 1990s and appeared to be some perversion of what education ought to be about. Teaching and testing became the focus rather than children and their learning and the enshrining of 'subjects' would prove to be 'the roots that clutch'. Many educationalists still cling with zealous tenacity to the historically and politically institutionalized 'subject' curriculum.

Our Common Curriculum began with the Education Reform Order in 1989: its implementation from 1991. Statutory Assessment was introduced in 1992, with teachers required to make assessments in English and mathematics, and Irish in Irish-medium schools, at the end of each Key Stage: at age eight, 11 and 14. By 1996, some revisions were made in terms of content since there was overwhelming concern about the amount to be covered. Until the late 1990s, however, any guidance about curriculum was in response to government directives in England; the Council for Curriculum, Examinations and Assessment (CCEA) and its predecessor bodies had little opportunity to be either proactive or innovative.

Through a process of monitoring and gathering information about what was and what was not working well in the curriculum, and a growing awareness of issues impinging on learning and teaching, evidence for the direction of change emerged. There were four planned and interrelated strands contributing to this.

1. Monitoring the views of young people

Research, commissioned by CCEA in 1996 and carried out by the National Foundation for Educational Research (NFER), focused initially on the end of Key Stage 2 and Key Stage 3 (11 to 14 year olds), but extended to the perceptions of pupils post-16. The study was unique because it explores the all-important voice of the learner:

> … out of all the countries which introduced national curricula in the early 1990s, it is only in Northern Ireland that you can find a significant attempt to evaluate the impact of the whole curriculum on learners. (Dr John Harland, director of the project, NFER 2002: from his speech at the launch of research findings)

This longitudinal cohort study involved tracking approximately 60 young people, over seven years, from the age of 11–18. Their insights were supported by questionnaire surveys of around 3,000 of their peers. The study's aims were centred on gathering evidence from pupils and teachers about the impact of the curriculum in terms of its relevance, breadth, balance, coherence, enjoyability and manageability. Five reports were produced from 1999–2004, revealing many negative perceptions from pupils and teachers about the impact of the curriculum. The overwhelming plea from pupils was to make learning relevant, connected and skills-based.

> It revealed a culture of compliance without engagement … The vast majority were of the view that schooling was relevant only for passing exams and jumping hurdles and had little relevance to young people's lives either now or in the future. (Carmel Gallagher, cited in CCEA, 2005)

Ironically, while it is widely accepted that the major justification for a 'National Curriculum' is that it offers a broad, balanced and common experience for all pupils, it was evident from the study's findings that the reality was somewhat different. Variety rather than commonality was on offer.

In terms of coherence, teachers in the study reported that cross-curricular links were serendipitous rather than deliberate. Tracking observations showed that pupils' days were strongly compartmentalized into a series of subject-based experiences with minimal opportunities for exploring links across subject areas. It is little wonder that, especially in grammar schools, pupils' perceptions of the worth of particular subjects were based on utilitarian values. It was also found, somewhat surprisingly, that there were significant levels of disengagement among high-attaining pupils as well as low-attaining ones.

It was also clear from the study that the exigency of academic selection at age 11 was skewing the curriculum in primary schools.

2. Monitoring teachers' views

During 1997 and 1998, teachers were consulted to ascertain their perceptions on the appropriateness of the current curriculum and on aspects to be addressed within the review of curriculum and assessment. There was a clear sense of frustration and, while teachers were not overwhelmingly happy with the existing curriculum, they did not feel overly enamoured with the prospect of more change. There was a feeling of having been disempowered and this would be acknowledged by CCEA in decisions taken about the nature and pace of the consultation, development and implementation of the revised curriculum.

3. Curriculum 21 conferences

During 1997/1998, CCEA organized a series of high-profile, thought-provoking conferences, aptly called 'Curriculum 21', where national and international researchers and practitioners in areas of learning, curriculum and the world of work, were brought together to 'provide a forum for constructive debate about the nature and structure of an appropriate curriculum for the 21st century' (CCEA, 1999).

The ten Curriculum 21 conferences explored areas such as new technologies, new forms of employment and work patterns, globalization of the market place, environmental change, the symbiosis of individual and societal development and the increasing knowledge about how we learn.

Key messages from the conferences and feedback from the monitoring programme were synthesized into a report and published by CCEA in 1999. Informed by the monitoring evidence, consultations with teachers, pupils and educational partners, and inspired by insights gleaned from Curriculum 21 conferences, CCEA was, for the first time, able to offer informed strategic advice about the curriculum and its assessment. With the establishment of a Northern Ireland Assembly, emanating from the 'Good Friday (Belfast) Agreement' in April 1998, the canvas for curriculum reform seemed to be a landscape overflowing with possibilities.

4. Consultation and debate

Early in 1999, CCEA gave advice to DoE in a paper, *Developing the Northern Ireland Curriculum to Meet the Needs of Young People, Society and the Economy in the 21st Century*, recommending that the curriculum and assessment arrangements should be reviewed. The advice outlined six objectives for the review of the curriculum, in relation to aims, skills, relevance, flexibility and coherence, assessment and the management of the change process. This was approved by DoE and in the autumn of 1999 the review process began. By April 2000, CCEA had published consultation documents on proposals for a revised curriculum for the Foundation Stage (pre-school, six year olds); Key Stage 1 (six to eight year olds); Key Stage 2 (eight to 11 year olds); Key Stage 3 (11 to 14 year olds) and Key Stage 4 (14 to 16 year olds).

The debate that ensued reignited the dichotomy and tension between the traditional structure asserted and sustained through ten years of our common curriculum and the challenges, complexities and uncertainties of twenty-first-century life in Northern Ireland. As momentum developed, there was a sweeping shift in orientation as the agenda flipped to learning rather than the specificity of subjects and content. Choice, diversity, creativity, learning for life, learning skills and capabilities were set to be heralded as the modern hegemony within a connected, holistic curriculum.

In June 2004, five years and three major consultations after CCEA issued initial advice regarding fundamental changes to the curriculum, the proposals for future curriculum and assessment arrangements were accepted by DoE.

The revised curriculum

1. The underpinning rationale: an epistemic model

Our understanding of the learning process has been illuminated through ongoing research and a synthesis of findings within the neuro, cognitive and social sciences. We have more knowledge about the nature of human learning and its importance to individuals, society and the economy than at any other time. Conventional views and hypotheses have been disputed: Perkins' insightful work on the learnability of intelligence and Gardner's argument that it is essentially meaningless to reduce intelligence to a single quotient, challenge long-held beliefs.

Learning, we now purport, is something we can shape, get better at, personalize; something we can add to, connect, think about. It is learning and the use we make of it that will drive our future economy and determine what kind of society we will have and what kind of people we become, and that has a poignant resonance in Northern Ireland.

Conceptions of knowledge and curriculum have changed too; the 'delivery' of prescribed subject content may have been adequate 50 years ago, but it is anathema in our post-modern society. The messages from the learners' perspective in the cohort study raised key questions about the what and how of our curriculum. Its focus and design have been informed and shaped by twenty-first-century expectations and updated models of learning and knowledge acquisition; the world has moved on.

It is an opportune time for us to realize a vision of learning and curriculum within an education system that is both relevant and innovative. Idealism is there, anticipation and culturally modest risk-taking in our uncertain political climate.

Of course, there is no completely right answer, as Louis MacNeice (in Auden, 1964) observes:

> *And if the world were black and white entirely*
> *... We might be surer where we wish to go*
> *Or again we might be merely*
> *Bored, but in brute reality there is no*
> *Road that is right entirely.*
> (page 65)

The challenge, however, is for strategic decision makers to be mindful of the exigent but crucial process of integrating and unifying fragmentary ideas; to ignore this is to allow the accelerating accumulation of information to distort rather than develop educational thinking.

2. Aims and objectives

The aims of the revised curriculum are:

> **To empower young people to achieve their potential and to make informed and responsible choices and decisions throughout their lives.**

It has three interdependent curricular objectives, which are to provide opportunities for each young person to develop as:

- *an individual:* including personal and mutual understanding, personal health, moral character and spiritual awareness;

- *a contributor to society:* including citizenship, cultural understanding, media awareness and ethical awareness;

- *a contributor to the economy and the environment:* including employability, economic awareness and environmental responsibility.

This provides the framework for curriculum design: a lens through which each component is focused and shaped.

To achieve these aims and objectives, agreed changes, incorporated into each Key Stage, include:

- more flexibility for schools to decide what is best for their pupils;

- more emphasis on developing children's thinking skills, and their ability to solve problems and handle information;

- making personal, social and health education a legal requirement;

- adding education about citizenship and employability to the curriculum;

- making sure that the connections between what is taught in different subjects are clearly visible where previously they have often been hidden;

- moving from assessment at intervals to assessment on an ongoing basis which updates the pupil profile and which assists the learning process (Alan Lennon, chairman of CCEA, 2004 press release at www.rewardinglearning.com).

3. Key components of the revised curriculum

Skills and capabilities

Throughout primary and post-primary education, there will be an emphasis on thinking skills and personal capabilities across all learning areas. The intention is to develop children's personal, interpersonal and learning skills and their ability to think both creatively and critically: the skills essential for work and life. Professor Carol McGuinness (Queen's University Belfast – QUB) and Dr Lynne Bianchi (Sheffield Hallam University) have worked on a framework for the progression of skills. These thinking skills and personal capabilities include:

- managing information

- thinking, problem solving and decision making

- being creative

- working with others

- self-management.

The skills' framework provides useful qualitative heuristic statements that will assist teachers in planning and assessing pupils' progress. The development of thinking skills has been given particular emphasis and this has been advanced by ongoing local research. The Activating Children's Thinking Skills (ACTS) project, directed by Professor Carol McGuinness, was funded initially by the Economic and Social Research Council; its ongoing development has been financed and supported by DoE, CCEA and Education and Library Boards (ELB).

Focused on eight to 11 year olds, the current project has involved a training programme for schools, over three years, from 2001–2004, and the collection of data from the 80 teachers and 1,300 pupils involved. The evaluation tracks pupils' academic achievements, their learning orientations and self-concepts as learners and problem solvers.

It is based on the premise that 'good thinking may have as much to do with creating a disposition to be a good thinker as it has to do with acquiring specific skills and strategies' (McGuinness, 1999: page 6).

Essential elements in the ACTS programme are:

- the identification of five major clusters of thinking skills: searching for meaning; thinking creatively; developing flexible and creative thinking; problem solving; decision making; and 'metacognition' which orchestrates, monitors and regulates them;

- explicit teaching of these specific thinking skills, where teachers and pupils are encouraged to develop a thinking vocabulary, taking time to reflect and talk about their thinking strategies;

- an infusion approach to embed and develop thinking skills across the curriculum;

- thinking diagrams which make the thinking process explicit.

The teachers involved in the project have contributed to the production of an ACTS handbook which contains training materials and teachers' lesson plans. These materials will be used by other teachers within the implementation of the revised curriculum. The approaches are appropriate for use throughout primary and post-primary schools.

Assessment for learning

There will also be a shift in focus to ongoing formative and integrated assessment with emphasis on pedagogy which scaffolds the learning process. The existing Key Stage assessment system will be replaced with one based on a statutory annual report, the pupil profile, and will provide parents with succinct indicators of their children's progress and achievements.

Since this assessment for learning culture may represent, for many teachers, a considerable shift in thinking about the functions and processes of assessment, its development is being supported by an ELB/CCEA Action Research Project.

The main purposes of the project, which is now entering Phase 2, are:

- to develop an increased level of awareness and expertise in assessment for learning (AfL);

- to form learning teams of teachers as action researchers;

- to develop 'home-grown' exemplar support materials;

- to provide a pool of 'teacher-trainers' with expertise, confidence and experience to lead developments in this aspect of the revised curriculum.

Learning networks have been set up to enable teachers to explore, discuss and develop authentic classroom practice. Key messages from research studies (Black and Wiliam, 1998, 1999; Clarke, 2001, 2003; Kohn, 1999; Dweck, 1999) are being interpreted by the teachers involved as they construct appropriate methodologies for developing assessment for learning in their classrooms. This will be an important element in the implementation process, forming a professional development package which will support the 'phasing in' of this learning and assessment culture.

Local and global citizenship

 It is in the shelter of each other that the people live.
(Is ar scáth a chéile a mhaireann na daoine.)

This well-known Irish proverb creates a powerful image of what we are striving for in Northern Ireland. Education for Mutual Understanding and Cultural Heritage were established as educational themes in 1992. The intention in introducing a programme of citizenship education is to build on this, acknowledging the responsibility that the education system has 'to contribute towards the maintenance of peace' (CCEA, 1999).

Local and global citizenship is now a distinctive strand within both primary and post-primary learning areas, with a strong emphasis on personal, interpersonal, thinking and communication skills and opportunities for pupils to examine individual, social and environmental responsibilities.

The importance of promoting citizenship can be fully appreciated in Northern Ireland society as it moves away from a culture of violence and avoidance that has characterized our lives for more than 30 years.

Supported by the United Nations Educational, Scientific and Cultural Organization (UNESCO) Centre at University of Ulster, citizenship development projects are being implemented and practical classroom materials produced to encourage young people to think about local and global challenges. 'Primary values' is one of the resources which, utilizing a 'community of enquiry' methodology, encourages reflection on different points of view, consideration of consequences and informed decision making. Through the powerful medium of story, its emphasis is on promoting a culture of tolerance in dealing with conflict, prejudice and human diversity.

Employability

The Department for Economic Development's *Strategy 2010* articulates a vision for our economy as:

> ... *a fast growing, competitive, innovative, knowledge based economy where there are plentiful opportunities and a population equipped to grasp them* (Department for Economic Strategy, 1999: Section 1, page 9)

Globalization and technology bring new opportunities and challenges. Articulated in the objectives of the revised curriculum, 'education for employability' is the means whereby young people will develop the appropriate skills, knowledge and attitudes to lifelong learning and the world of work. At KS1 and 2, employability is catered for within the personal development strand of the curriculum, under the theme of 'living in the local and wider community'. At KS3 and 4 it is embedded in 'learning for life and work'.

Schools are being encouraged to work in partnership with the business world, through a range of projects designed to develop a culture which values creativity, entrepreneurship and enterprise, and opportunities to experience the 'real' working community.

4. Key features in primary education

Throughout the primary phase, the revised curriculum will be more holistic, with emphasis on developing children's skills, capabilities and the capacity to learn for themselves. It is set out in learning areas rather than subjects, with integration and linkages important. The ending of academic selection will allow greater flexibility for teachers to follow the interests of children and for the content to be more appropriate and motivating. A greater emphasis is given to personal development, which includes personal understanding, health, mutual understanding and living in the local and wider community. There has been particular focus on the relevance of the curriculum in the early years.

A good start

The new Foundation Stage represents a major shift in thinking within our traditional system. In Northern Ireland, many children enter formal education at age four. It has long been recognized that some of these very young children, especially boys, are not developmentally ready for the demands made in their first year at school, with 'failure' evident within a few months of starting formal education. It seems bizarre that a generously funded 'reading recovery' programme is provided for those children who have 'failed' in reading as they enter their second year at school.

'The early years' enriched curriculum' began in 2000 with a group of six schools in Greater Shankill, a 'disadvantaged' area of Belfast. Its aim was to promote an innovative, developmentally appropriate curriculum for Year 1 and Year 2 children; its fundamental goal to foster self-esteem and positive attitudes to learning as a foundation to formal education.

The 'enriched curriculum' has been developed and extended to other less disadvantaged areas. Emphasis is on play, the promotion of personal and social skills, independence, self-regulation, oral language skills and motor development. Children's emergent writing, literacy and numeracy activity is valued and there is flexibility in introducing children to formal schemes when the child is ready for the scheme rather than the other way round. Teachers have benefited from DoE funding and networking opportunities.

An evaluation of the project has been carried out by QUB and Stranmillis University College. Interim feedback has indicated that the children:

- show more rapid development in talking, listening and mathematics;

- despite a later start to formal instruction in reading and writing, quickly begin to make up the ground;

- show evidence of greater self-confidence and self-esteem, with noticeably fewer attention-span problems;

- show evidence of a more positive attitude to reading and to books in general. (CCEA, 2004, page 9)

It is also evident that this approach is helping to close the gap between boys and girls.

5. Key features in post-primary education

Building on the research into the effects of our selective system, an independent review body, chaired by Gerry Burns, was set up to widely consult on post-primary issues. The Burns' Report, 2001 emphasized inclusion and amelioration of the effects of social deprivation and presented the main issues from the public consultation, outlining three key integral innovations:

- The development of a pupil profile with information on a wide range of attributes and achievements.

- The abolition of transfer tests and academic selection.

- The creation of local collaborative networks of schools in a system of collegiates.

This was followed by a working group, chaired by Steve Costello, which took account of the consultation feedback. The Costello Report detailed findings from extensive studies of alternative systems and offered coherent and controversial arguments for extending the opportunities for all young people. Accepted in 2004, the recommendations include:

- Access to a curriculum entitlement framework for all pupils, with a much wider range of choices – vocational and academic.

- New transfer arrangements, with the intention to end the current selection transfer procedure by 2008.

The new post-primary arrangements will include access for all pupils to a curriculum entitlement framework and transfer from primary school based on informed parental choice rather than transfer procedure tests, ending academic selection at 11. These arrangements are being implemented as one element of an integrated approach, called 'entitled to succeed'. Also intended are collaborative workings between schools, the establishment of specialist schools and the provision of a more holistic, connected curriculum, with specific emphasis on real-world skills and on learning which is appropriate for life and work:

> *Pupils must be able to access courses that genuinely interest them and are of value. The menu of choice must therefore be as rich and varied as we can reasonably make it.* (Gardner, 2004: page 17)

Learning for life and work within an entitlement framework will provide each young person with access to a guaranteed minimum number and range of courses: Costello recommended 24 courses at KS4 and 27 courses post-16, with at least a third of a vocational or applied nature. The flexibility initiative is already underway, allowing schools to discontinue aspects of the statutory curriculum and to introduce pupils in years 11 and 12 to innovative work-related learning programmes.

6. Teacher involvement

 Educational change depends on what teachers do and think – it's as simple and as complex as that.

(Fullan, 1991: page 117)

Progress in education is inevitably bound up with teacher development. Since this is a curriculum that cannot be neatly packaged, compartmentalized, delivered and assessed, the challenges of sustainable implementation cannot be met in a spirit of more of the same. Crucially, unlike previous initiatives, the changes in the revised curriculum are not about 'tagging on' additional elements since this would lead to increased pressure and frustration in schools. Sustainability, according to Hargreaves and Fink (2000):

> *... does not simply mean whether something can last. It addresses how particular initiatives can be developed without compromising the development of others in the surrounding environment now and in the future.* (pages 30–34)

Reduced, integrated content and greater flexibility will allow for the development of 'new' aspects such as the focus on personal development, skills and capabilities, citizenship and employability.

Given that the common curriculum of 1999 was foisted on them it was important to ensure that teachers had a stake in the development of the revised curriculum. They have been encouraged to be active agents in the production and dissemination of an emerging pedagogic discourse through research projects, and through the piloting and development of materials. Building a dynamic professional community has been a priority: the 'teacher-proof' curriculum of the early 1990s has given way to 'teacher-led' curriculum development.

CCEA, working in partnership with ELBs, is encouraging and enabling teachers to reflect on practices and engage in mediated enquiry and to disseminate authentic practice through written case studies, DVDs, locally produced resources and 'showcase' events.

Classroom 2000 (C2K) established within the Education Technology Strategy for Northern Ireland (DENI, 1997) has impacted significantly both on teacher development and curriculum development. C2K is responsible for the provision of an information, communications and technology managed service to all schools. A major technological infastructure, it is the largest online education system in the world, involving 40,000 networked computers, over 1,200 schools, 330,000 pupils and almost 20,000 teachers. It is currently developing its managed learning environment, 'Learning Northern Ireland', which offers a fully integrated service that will provide schools with online access to an increasingly sophisticated range of curricular and assessment resource materials.

Conclusion

Politically, our conciliatory paths have been characterized by meandering and cul-de-sacs; developments in our education system, while less nebulous, also suffer from congealed thinking. The change journey has not been without turbulence; clouds have often blocked the sun.

Real, lasting change will happen when vision, curriculum and pedagogy merge within an education structure that is designed to nurture the fusion. The aims and values embedded in the revised curriculum do not sit comfortably within the current differentiated and segregated education system but an agreed alternative is still a little obscure. The continuing enigma of a replacement for 'selection' at 11 and the lack of clarity and somewhat volatile debate on the proposals for the change in post-primary education have led to much ambiguity and frustration. The success of our revised curriculum will depend on the degree of congruence in the system and there is much to be unravelled there.

There is also concern about the funding implications of the changes: an enriched curriculum in the Foundation Stage; ongoing professional development of teachers; the provision of an increased number of subjects at Key Stage 4; and concomitant teacher expertise, school inter-workings and the development of specialist schools. Each requires the investment of significant additional resources; funding, or lack of it, could prove to be a major stumbling block.

The precarious status of our local assembly and the widespread feelings of insecurity abounding within the current review of public administration add to the uncertainty in the change process. But, having held to our beliefs with heron-like patience, we remain committed to escaping the deadening effect of the old obsession with inappropriate standards, measures and subject straitjackets. Our compelling vision is to develop individuals who have a desire and disposition to learn, live, work and contribute to our communities, society, economic growth and environmental improvement.

At this point, we recognize that, in the midst of difficulty and volatility, we have crossed the threshold; the ineluctable tide of change has swept us to a 'tipping point':

 It may seem an immovable, implacable place … With the slightest push, in just the right place, it can be tipped.

(Gladwell, 2001: page 259)

The 'roll-out' of the revised curriculum will go ahead through a phased, supported and collaborative implementation strategy, with 2007 set as a starting date. We hope that its realization will do justice to the commitment and visionary insights of those who have influenced and shaped the changes; intuitively we know that it will.

We go back to our cultural roots in asserting, as Heaney does, that 'Learning's easy carried'. We have seized the unique opportunity in Northern Ireland: our imminent, if somewhat elusive, devolved government, our population size and, crucially, our widespread determination to nurture our children and our future, within a relevant, radical and rich curriculum, will ensure that their learning is 'easily carried'. The idea of lifelong learning is powerful, its promise and endurability expressed, as Heaney (1991) continues his poem:

 The bag is light,
Scuffed and supple and unemptiable.

References and acknowledgements

All extracts in this book are reproduced with permission of the publisher. Acknowledgements are made at the end of the relevant reference.

Every effort has been made to contact copyright holders of materials reproduced in this book. The publishers apologize for any omissions and will be pleased to rectify them at the earliest opportunity.

Ackling, S. and Lowes, K. (2004) *Thriving in the Digital Networked Economy*, British Telecom position paper, BT, London.

Adonis, A. and Pollard, S. (1997) *A Class Act: The Myth of Britain's Classless Society*, Penguin, London. (Reproduced with permission of Penguin and Curtis Brown; © Andrew Adonis and Stephen Pollard)

Alexander, J., Daly, P., Gallagher, A., Gray, C. and Sutherland, A. (1998) *An Evaluation of the Craigavon Two-tier System*, DENI, Bangor.

Argyris, C. and Schön, D. (1974) *Theory in Practice: Increasing Professional Effectiveness*, Jossey-Bass, San Francisco, Calif. (Reproduced with permission of John Wiley & Sons, Inc.)

Armstrong, T. (2000) *Multiple Intelligences in the Classroom*, 2nd edn, Association for Curriculum Development, Alexandria, Va.

Assessment is for Learning *Project 1* www.ltscotland.org.uk/assess/projects_project_1_conf2_vignette_e.asp, Learning and Teaching, Scotland.

Auden, W.H. (ed.) (1964) *Selected Poems of Louis MacNeice*, Faber and Faber, London. (Reproduced with permission of David Higham Associates)

Barthe, R.S. (2001) *Learning by Heart*, Jossey-Bass, San Francisco, Calif.

Becta (2003) *What Research Says about ICT and Motivation Report*, Becta, Coventry.

Bentley, T. and Wilsden, J. (eds) (2003) *The Adaptive State*, Demos, London.

Black, P. (1998) *Testing: Friend or Foe? Theory and Practice of Assessment and Testing*, Falmer Press, London. (Reproduced with permission of Falmer Press/Thomson Publishing)

Black. P., Harrison, C., Lee, C., Marshall, B. and Wiliam, D. et al. (2002) *Working Inside the Black Box: Assessment for Learning in the Classroom*, Department of Education and Professional Studies, King's College, London.

Black, P. and Wiliam, D. (1998) 'Review Article', *Assessment in Education*, Vol. 5, No. 1.

Black, P. and Wiliam, D. (1999) *Beyond the Black Box*, School of Education, Cambridge.

Bloom, B. (1984) 'The 2 Sigma Problem: the Search for Methods of a Group Instruction as Effective as One-to-One Tutoring', *Educational Researcher*, June/July: 4–16.

Bowring-Carr, C. and West-Burnham, J. (1997) *Effective Learning in Schools*, Pearson Education, London. (Reproduced with permission of Pearson Education Ltd)

Broadfoot, P., Claxton, G. and Deakin Crick, R. (2005) *The Effective Lifelong Learning Inventory*, www.bristol.ac.uk/education/enterprise/elli

Brown, M.M. (2000) *Bringing Information Affluence to the Developing World*, Address to the State of the World Forum, New York, 7 September.

Bryk, A. and Schneider, B. (2002) *Trust in Schools: A Core Resource for Improvement*, Russell Sage Foundation, New York. (Reprinted with permission of Russell Sage Foundation, 112 East 64th Street, New York, NY 10021)

Burns, G. (2001) *Education for the 21st Century*, Report by the Post-Primary Review Body, Department of Education, Bangor.

Buzan T. (1996) *The Mind Map Book: How to Use Radiant Thinking to Maximize Your Brain's Untapped Potential*, Plume, New York.

Capra, F. (2002) *The Hidden Connections*, HarperCollins, London. (Reprinted with permission of HarperCollins Publishers Ltd and Brockman Inc.)

Carter, R. (1998) *Mapping the Mind*, Weidenfeld & Nicolson, London. (Reproduced with permission of Weidenfeld & Nicolson, an imprint of The Orion Publishing Group)

CCEA (1999) *Developing the Northern Ireland Curriculum to Meet the Needs of Young People, Society and the Economy in the 21st Century*, CCEA, Belfast. (Reproduced with permission of Carmel Gallagher)

CCEA (2004) *Way Ahead Primary*, CCEA, Belfast.

Ceci, S.J. (1990) *On Intelligence, More or Less: A Biological Treatise on Intellectual Development*, Harvard University Press, Cambridge, Mass.

Clarke, S. (2001) *Unlocking Formative Assessment*, Hodder & Stoughton, London.

Clarke, S. (2003) *Enriching Feedback*, Hodder & Stoughton, London.

Claydon, L.F. (1969) *Rousseau*, Collier Macmillan, London.

Coates, M. (1999) 'Jewels in a Lead Coronet' in Bowring-Carr, C. and West-Burnham, J. (eds) *Managing Learning for Achievement*, Financial Times, London.

Coffield, F.C., Mosely, D.M., Hall, E. and Ecclestone, K. (2004) *Should we be Using Learning Styles? What Research has to Say to Practice. Learning Styles and Pedagogy in Post-16 Learning Report B*, Learning and Skills Development Agency, London.

Collins, A.M. and Quillian, M.R. (1969) 'Retrieval Time from Semantic Memory', *Journal of Verbal Learning and Verbal Behaviour*, Vol. 8, 240–247.

Conner, M. and Hodgins, W. (2000) *Learning Styles*,www.learnativity.com/learningstyles.html

Cooperrider, D.L., Whitney, D. and Stavros, J. (2003) *Appreciative Inquiry Handbook*, Lakeshore Publishers, Bedford Heights, Oh. (Reproduced with permission of David L. Cooperrider)

Corvi, R. (1997) *An Introduction to the Thoughts of Karl Popper*, Routledge, London. (Reproduced with permission of Thomson Publishing)

Cox, M. (1997) *The Effects of Information Technology on Students' Motivation: Final Report*, King's College London, School of Education, London.

Csikszentmihalyi, M. (1997) *Finding Flow*, Basic Books, New York. (Reproduced with permission of Perseus Books)

Department for Education and Employment (1999) *All Our Futures: Creativity, Culture and Education: The National Advisory Committee's Report*, HMSO, London. Available on www.developmentgateway.org

Department for Education and Skills (2004a) *Personalised Learning*, www.standards.dfes.gov.uk

Department for Education and Skills (2004b) *A National Conversation about Personalised Learning*, DfES, London.

Department of Economic Development (1999) *Strategy 2010: A Report by the Economic Development Strategy Review Steering Group*, Department of Economic Development, Bangor.

Department of Education for Northern Ireland (1997) *A Strategy for Education Technology in Northern Ireland*, DENI, Bangor.

Desforges, C. (2003) *The Impact of Parental Involvement, Parental Support and Family Education on Pupil Achievements and Adjustment: A Literature Review*, DfES, London.

Development Gateway (2005) www.developmentgateway.org

Duckworth, J. (2001) Notschool.netresearch phase – final report www.notschool.net/what/pubs/pdf/final report.pdf

Dweck, C. (1999) *Self-Theories: Their Role in Motivation, Personality and Development*, Psychology Press, Philadelphia, Pa.

Eccles, J. (1996) *The Brain and the Unity of Conscious Experience*, Arthur Stanly Eddigton Memorial Lectures No. 19, Cambridge University Press, Cambridge. (Reproduced with permission of Cambridge University Press)

Edgar, D. (2001) *The Patchwork Nation*, HarperCollins, Sydney. (Reproduced with permission of HarperCollins Publishers)

Entwistle, N. (1992) *The Impact of Teaching and Learning Outcomes in Higher Education*, CVCP, Staff Development Unit, Sheffield.

Everard, K.B. and Morris, G. (1996) *Effective School Management*, 3rd edn, Paul Chapman, London. (Reproduced with permission of Sage Publications Ltd)

Field, J. (2003) *Social Capital*, Routledge, London. (Reproduced with permission of Thomson Publishing)

Forster, E.M. (1909) *The Machine Stops* in Zimmerman, H. (ed.) *Aspects of E.M. Forster.* Available on http://emforster.de/

Freire, P. (1998) *Pedagogy of Freedom*, trans. Macedo, D., Rowman & Littlefield Publishers, Lanham, Md. (Reproduced with permission of Rowman & Littlefield Publishers, Inc.)

Fukuyama, F. (1995) *Trust: The Social Virtues and the Creation of Prosperity*, The Free Press, New York. (Reproduced with permission of Simon & Schuster Adult Publishing Group and International Creative Management. © Francis Fukuyama)

Fullan, M. (1991) *The New Meaning of Educational Change*, Cassell, London. (Reproduced with permission of Cassell, The Continuum International Publishing Group)

Gallagher, T. and Smith, A. (2000) *The Effects of the Selective System of Secondary Education in Northern Ireland*, Department of Education, Bangor.

Gardner, H. (1983) *Frames of Mind: The Theory of Multiple Intelligence*, Fontana Press, London. (Reproduced with permission of HarperCollins Publishers Ltd)

Gardner, H. (1999a) *Intelligence Reframed, Multiple Intelligences for the 21st Century*, Basic Books, New York. (Reproduced with permission of Perseus Books)

Gardner, H. (1999b) *The Disciplined Mind: What all Students should Understand*, Simon & Schuster, New York. (Reproduced with permission of Simon & Schuster Adult Publishing Group and Fish & Richardson. © Howard Gardner)

Gardner, H. (2004) *Entitled to Succeed*, Newsletter, Department of Education, Bangor.

Gipps, C.V. (1994) *Beyond Testing, Towards a Theory of Educational Assessment*, Falmer Press, London. (Reproduced with permission of Thomson Publishing)

Gipson, S. (2003) *Issues of ICT, School Reform and Learning-Centred School Design*, Practitioner Enquiry Report, NCSL, Nottingham. (Reproduced with permission of S. Gipson)

Gladwell, M. (2001) *The Tipping Point – How Little Things Can Make a Big Difference*, Abacus, London. (Reproduced with permission of Time Warner Book Group UK and Janklow & Nesbitt Associates)

Goleman, D. (1996) *Emotional Intelligence: Why It Can Matter More than IQ*, Bloomsbury, London.

Goleman, D. (1998) *Working with Emotional Intelligence*, Bloomsbury Publishing, London. (Reproduced with permission of Bloomsbury and Random House, Inc.)

Goleman, D. (2002) *The New Leaders*, Little, Brown, London. (Reproduced with permission of Time Warner Book Group UK and Brockman Inc.)

Greenfield, S. (2000) *Brain Story*, BBC Worldwide Limited, London. (Reproduced with permission of BBC Worldwide Limited. © Susan Greenfield)

Gregorc, A.F. (1982) *Gregorc Style Delineator™: A Self-assessment Instrument for Adults*, Gregorc Associates, Inc., Columbia, Conn.

Grinder, M. (1989) *Righting the Educational Conveyor Belt*, Metamorphous Press, Portland, Oreg. (Reproduced with permission of Metamorphous Press, Portland, OR 97296-0616)

Handy, C. (1994) *The Empty Raincoat*, BCA Hutchinson, London. (Reproduced with permission of The Random House Group Ltd and Harvard Business School Press)

Hargreaves, A. and Fink, D. (2000) 'The Three Dimensions of Reform', *Educational Leadership*, Vol. 57, No. 7: 30–34. (Reproduced with permission of ASCD; The Association for Supervision and Curriculum Development is a worldwide community of educators advocating sound policies and sharing best practices to achieve the success of each learner. To learn more, visit ASCD at www.ascd.org)

Hargreaves, D. (2004) *Personalising Learning*, Specialist Schools Trust, London. (Reproduced with permission of Davis Hargreaves)

Harlen, W. and Deakin Crick, R. (2002) 'A Systematic Review of the Impact of Summative Assessment and Tests on Students' Motivation for Learning' (EPPI-Centre Review), *Research Evidence in Education Library*, Issue 1, London: EPPI-Centre, Social Science Research Unit, Institute of Education. Available at http://eppi.ioe.ac.uk/EPPIWeb/home.aspx?page=/reel/review_groups/assessment/review_one.htm

Heaney, S. (1991) 'The Schoolbag' in *Seeing Things*, Faber & Faber, London. (Reproduced with permission of Faber & Faber)

Hirschhorn, L. (1997) *Reworking Authority*, MIT Press, Cambridge, Mass. (Reproduced with permission of The MIT Press)

Hutton, W. (1996) *The State We're In*, Jonathan Cape, London. (Reproduced with permission of The Random House Group Ltd)

Huxley, A. (1932) *Brave New World*, Vintage Classics, London. (Reproduced with permission of The Estate of Aldous Huxley)

Jensen, E. (1998) *Teaching with the Brain in Mind*, ASCD, Alexandria, Va. (Reproduced with permission of ASCD; The Association for Supervision and Curriculum Development is a worldwide community of educators advocating sound policies and sharing best practices to achieve the success of each learner. To learn more, visit ASCD at www.ascd.org)

Jonassen, D. (2000) *Computers as Mindtools for Schools: Engaging Critical Thinking*, Prentice Hall, Upper Saddle River, NJ.

Kendler, K.S., Gardener, C.O. and Prescott, C.A. (1998) 'A Population Based Twin Study of Self-esteem and Gender', *Psychological Medicine*, Vol. 28: 1403–1409.

Kirriemuir, J. and McFarlane, L. (2004) *Literature Review in Games and Learning*, Report 8, Nesta Futurelab, Bristol. (Reproduced with permission of nestafuturelab.org)

Kohn, A. (1999) *Punished by Rewards*, Houghton Mifflin, Boston, Mass.

Lackney, J. (2001) *Classrooms of the Future, Thinking out of the Box*, an invited paper presentation given at the Ninth Annual Michigan Educational Facilities Conference, Shanty Creek's Summit Conference Center.

Leadbeater, C. (2004) *Learning about Personalisation*, DfES Publications, Nottingham.

Lennon, A. (2004) Press release, www.rewardinglearning.com/

Loveless, A. and Wegerif, R. (2004) 'Creativity and ICT' in Williams, M. and Fisher, R. (pre-print draft).

Lynas, M. (2004) *High Tide: News from a Warming World*, Flamingo, London. (Reproduced with permission of HarperCollins Publishers Ltd)

MacLeod, R. (ed.) (1982) *Days of Judgment: Science Examinations and the Organisation of Knowledge in Late Victorian England*, Nafferton Books, Driffield. (Reproduced with permission of Nafferton Books)

Manhattan High Schools Superintendency (2002) *Assessing the Reliability of Websites*, www.mediaworkshop.org/mhss

McCombs, B.L. (1999) *Learner-centred Classroom Practices*. Available from the author. University of Denver Research Institute, Denver, Colo.

McGuinness, C. (1999) *From Thinking Skills to Thinking Classrooms: A Review and Evaluation of Approaches for Developing Pupils' Thinking*, Research Report No. 115 for DfEE, London.

McLean, A. (2003) *The Motivated School*, Paul Chapman Publishing, London. (Reproduced with permission of Sage Publications Ltd)

Mercer, N. (2004) *The Guided Construction of Knowledge*, Multilingual Matters Ltd, Clevedon. (Reproduced with permission of Multilingual Matters Ltd)

Mosely, D. and Higgins, S. (1999) *Ways Forward with ICT: Effective Pedagogy Using Information and Communications Technology for Literacy and Numeracy in Primary Schools*, www.ncl.ac.uk/ecls/research/project_ttaict/ttaict1.htm

Neuberger, J. (2005) *The Moral State We're In*, HarperCollins, London. (Reproduced with permission of HarperCollins Publishers and Gillon Aitken Associates Ltd. © Julia Neuberger)

Newman, J. (2002) 'The New Public Management, Modernization and Institutional Change' in McLaughlin, K., Osborne, P. and Ferlie, E. (eds) *New Public Management*, Routledge, London.

Office for Standards in Education (2004) *ICT in Schools: The Impact of Government Initiatives Five Years On*, HMI, London.

O'Neill, O. (2002) *A Question of Trust*, Cambridge University Press, Cambridge. (Reproduced with permission of Cambridge University Press)

Papert, S. (1980) *Mindstorms: Children, Computers, and Powerful Ideas*, Basic Books, New York. (Reproduced with permission of Perseus Books)

Pask, G. (1976) 'Styles and Strategies of Learning', *British Journal of Psychology*, Vol. 46, No. II: 128–148.

Pea, R.D. (1997) 'Practices of Distributed Intelligence and Designs for Education' in Salomon, G. (ed.) *Distributed Cognitions*, Cambridge University Press, Cambridge. (Reproduced with permission of Cambridge University Press)

Perkins, D. (1992) *Smart Schools: Better Thinking and Learning for Every Child*, The Free Press, New York. (Reproduced with permission of The Free Press, a Division of Simon & Schuster Adult Publishing Group. and Fish & Richardson. © David Perkins)

Pinker, S. (2002) *The Blank Slate*, Penguin, London. (Reproduced with permission of Viking Penguin, a division of Penguin Group (USA) Inc., and Brockman Inc.)

Power, S., Warren, S., Gillborn, D., Clark, A., Thomas, S. and Coate, K. (2002) *Education in Deprived Areas: Outcomes, Inputs and Processes*, Institute of Education, London. (Reproduced with permission of the authors)

Prior, G. and Hall, L. (2004) *ICT in Schools Survey 2004*, Department for Education and Skills, London.

Putnam, R. (2000) *Bowling Alone*, Simon & Schuster, New York. (Reproduced with permission of University of Chicago Press)

Qualifications and Curriculum Authority (1998) www.qca.org.uk/futures (Reproduced with permission of QCA)

Qualifications and Curriculum Authority (2004a) *Financial Modelling of the English Exams System 2003–04*, QCA, London. (Reproduced with permission of QCA)

Qualifications and Curriculum Authority (2004b) *Designing a Personalised Curriculum for Alternative Provision at Key Stage 4*, QCA, Sudbury.

Rawls, J. (2001) *Justice as Fairness: A Restatement*, ed. Kelly, E., The Belknap Press of Harvard University Press, Cambridge, Mass. (Reproduced with permission of the President and Fellows of Harvard College)

Resnick, L.B. and Resnick, D.P. (1992) 'Assessing the Thinking Curriculum: New Tools for Educational Reform' in Gifford, B. and O'Connor, M. (eds) *Changing Assessments: Alternative Views of Aptitude, Achievement and Instruction*, Kluwer Academic Publishers, London. (Reproduced with permission of Springer Science and Business Media)

Ridley, M. (1999) *Genome: The Autobiography of a Species in 23 Chapters*, Fourth Estate, London. (Reproduced with permission HarperCollins Publishers Ltd)

Ridley, M. (2003) *Nature via Nurture*, HarperCollins, London. (Reproduced with permission of HarperCollins Publishers Ltd and Curtis Brown Ltd)

Sachs, J. (2003) *The Dignity of Difference*, Continuum, London. (Reproduced with permission of The Continuum International Publishing Group)

Sadler, R. (1989) 'Formative Assessment and the Design of Instructional Systems', *Instructional Science,* Vol. 18: 119–144.

Sergiovanni, T. J. (2001) *Leadership: What's in it for Schools?*, RoutledgeFalmer, London. (Reproduced with permission of Thomson Publishing)

Shaw, M. and Paton, G. (2004) 'Bespoke Plans Suit Heads', *TES*, 15 October. (Reproduced with permission of *TES*)

Shepard, L. (1991) 'Psychometricians' Beliefs About Learning' *Educational Researcher*, Vol. 20, No. 7.

Shepard, L. (1992) 'What Policy Makers who Mandate Tests Should Know About the New Psychology of Intellectual Ability and Learning' in Gifford, B. and O'Connnor, M. (eds) *Changing Assessments: Alternative Views of Aptitude, Achievement and Instruction*, Kluwer Academic Publishers, London. (Reproduced with permission of L. Shepard)

Sizer, T.R. and Sizer, N.F. (1999) *The Students are Watching: Schools and the Moral Contract*, Beacon Press, Boston, Mass. (Reproduced with permission of Beacon Press)

Southworth, G. (2004) *How Leaders Influence What Happens in Classrooms*, NCSL, Nottingham. (Reproduced with permission of Geoff Southworth)

Stanford University (2003) Enumclaw High School, www.schoolredesign.net

Steiner, G. (2003) *Lessons of the Masters*, Harvard University Press, Cambridge, Mass. (Reproduced with permission of Harvard University Press. © George Steiner)

Sternberg, R.J. (1990) *Metaphors of Mind*, Cambridge University Press, Cambridge. (Reproduced with permission of Cambridge University Press)

Sternberg, R.J. (1999) *Intelligence*, http://psych.nwu.edu

TES (2002) 'Why is it Good to Talk?', 5 July. (Reproduced with permission of *TES*)

TES (2003) 'Are your Reports Bland and Useless?', 7 March. (Reproduced with permission of *TES*)

Toffler, A. (1970) *Future Shock*, Bodley Head, London. (Reproduced with permission of The Random House Group Ltd and A.P. Watt Ltd)

Torrance, H. (1993) *Can Testing Really Raise Educational Standards?*, IOT, Manchester Metropolitan University, Manchester, www.enquirylearning.net/ELU/issues/education/h.tassess.html

Veen, W. (2002) *Homo Zappiens*, presentation to NCSL, Nottingham. (Reproduced with permission of Wim Veen)

Wegerif, R. (2003) 'Can Computers Help Children to Think?' in Wiliams, S. (ed.) *Teaching Thinking*, Grillford, Milton Keynes. (Reproduced with permission of Grillford)

Weiss, D. (2003) *Going Online: Youth and the Internet*, Report for The Kaiser Family Foundation, New York.

West-Burnham, J. (2002) *Interpersonal Leadership*, NCSL, Nottingham.

Wheatley, M.J. (1992) *Leadership and the New Science*, Berrett-Koehler Publishers, San Francisco, Calif. (Reproduced with permission of Berrett-Koehler Publishers, Inc., www.bkconnection.com)

White, J. (1998) 'Do Howard Gardner's Multiple Intelligences Add Up?', *Perspectives on Education Policy*, Institute of Education, London.

Winston, R. (2003) *The Human Mind*, Bantam Press, London. (Reproduced with permission of The Random House Group Ltd)

Zohar, D. (1997) *Reviving the Corporate Brain*, Berrett-Koehler, San Francisco, Calif. (Reproduced with permission of Berrett-Koehler Publishers, Inc., www.bkconnection.com)

Zohar, D. and Marshall, I. (2000) *Spiritual Intelligence: The Ultimate Intelligence*, Bloomsbury Publishing, London.

Index